I0488292

CORPORATE MERGERS AND ACQUISITIONS: A Case Study

Charles Addo

Writers Club Press

San Jose New York Lincoln Shanghai

Corporate Mergers And Acquisitions: A Case Study

All Rights Reserved © 2000 by Charles Addo

No part of this book may be reproduced or transmitted in
any form or by any means, graphic, electronic, or mechanical,
including photocopying, recording, taping, or by any
information storage or retrieval system, without the
permission in writing from the publisher.

Published by Writers Club Press
an imprint of iUniverse.com, Inc.

For information address:
iUniverse.com, Inc.
620 North 48th Street
Suite 201
Lincoln, NE 68504-3467
www.iuniverse.com

ISBN: 0-595-00752-X

Printed in the United States of America

Dedicated with Love to:
my deceased father, James Addo, mother,
Mary Brefo-Inkum,
the memory of Godfrey Inkum,
daughters Mavis, Judith, Lizzie, Lisa, Stephanie,
and to Gifty Okwan Amoah and Agatha Appiah.

Contents

Chapter III
The Acquisition Process And
The Emergence Of Rival Bidder For Control Of Paramount

Chapter IV
The Financial And Non-Financial
Considerations Apparent In The Paramount-Viacom Action

Chapter V
Analysis Of The Price Offered By Viacom To Acquire Paramount

Chapter VI
Viacom Incorporation's Financial
Condition Before, During, And After

Chapter VII
Post-Acquisition Analysis Of Viacom And The Industry

Chapter VIII
The Future Of The Entertainment And Information Industry

Preface

A noted college professor and author of twelve books, once confided to this writer about the circumstances that led him into writing his first textbook: the prescribed textbook he used while a student did not explain the subject adequately enough to him. Today, that book he wrote is a standard text in use throughout institutions of higher learning in India and several countries.

This book has developed from this author's college term papers and capstone projects. It is about corporate mergers and acquisitions. Undoubtedly, the extent to which the activities of businesses affect society, and for that matter, the lives of individuals may, in the very least, be described as profound. The actions of corporations, both domestically and internationally, have a direct relationship to the quality of life of individuals through a web of complex and threatening interrelationships. When in the final analysis those actions turn out well, society reaps rewards of economic prosperity. Conversely, when those actions go awry, society reaps punitive repercussions.

During the 1980s, one such activity of corporations that became a conspicuous feature of the United States' economy was mergers and acquisitions. Mergers can affect all aspects of organizations: structure, processes, controls, management styles, motivation, and careers. These corporate activities involved several billions of dollars, and exacted heavy human toll on the labor force, particularly dislocated workers, and in some cases the effects were quite extreme. Today, these activities do not appear to show any decline, as evidenced by the recent Daimler

Benz-Chrysler, Viacom-CBS, and Time Warner-America On Line mergers, to mention only a few that come to mind.

Reports and rumors of acquisitions played a major role in hiking the Dow Jones Industrial Average to all-time highs in 1990 following the stock crash of October,1987. In this case, the results of corporate actions were quite favorable to society, and reaped a reward of economic prosperity. But the reward of economic prosperity may not always be the case. In fact, probing questions have already been raised about the potential adverse effects of mergers and acquisitions activities on the United States economy, and of course their rippling effects on the global economy, which may have their roots from the mergers and acquisitions activities of the 1990s. These concerns run the whole gamut from macroeconomic effects to the impacts on corporate equity shareholders.

By examining the acquisition of Paramount Communications by Viacom Incorporation, a transaction which was consummated in 1994, thus allowing enough elapsed time for significant evaluation to be made about the economic prudence of the transaction, this book enables the reader who seeks to get to the core of the intriguing subject of mergers and acquisitions to do so quickly without having to delve into the vast expanse of the subject.

But almost all textbooks these days are written by people with high level of expertise, people who often hold terminal degrees in their fields. Although, these books are well-intentioned and professionally thorough in their coverage of their subject matter, nevertheless, they often overlook a very important aspect in the knowledge transmission process. What then is this often overlooked aspect? Because these books are written by experts at the pinnacle of their expertise for "student experts," the very excellence of their expertise blinds them to the real needs of these "student experts."

It is against this backdrop that it is felt this timely book fills a void in the knowledge transmission process. For not only does this book attempts to make meaningful contribution to the store of knowledge of the intriguing subject of mergers and acquisitions with high degree of thoroughness, but perhaps most importantly, with the subject researched and written in-school as part of graduate school capstone project, it offers a more student-friendly overtone; just what students want to see.

In this way, it is felt that the aspiring expert on the subject, that is, the "student expert," often under the blues when it comes time to present his or her research project will be provided with a helpful companion that he or she can better relate to.

April, 2000   Charles Addo

                                                   Bronx, NY

Acknowledgements

This book would not have been possible without the research and published works of several people. But it is impossible for me to acknowledge individually the countless men and women whose ideas and research findings have contributed to making this book a reality. I am very much indebted to them.

However, a number of college professors and friends deserve to be mentioned here for their special help during the thoughts and the actual preparation of this book. I would like to thank Dr. Tom Milton, Chair of the Mercy College business administration department, for his guidance, support, and expertise which were freely placed at my disposal; Professor Wayne Cioffari, Dean of Mercy College MBA program for his critiques and helpful comments during the selection of my research topic that has now led to this book.

I also wish to thank Dr. Michael Cavanaugh of Mercy College for his great support towards my academic pursuit, Dr. N.P. Loomba of the Long Island University for his immense guidance during the writing of the research outline; and Professor Greg George of Mercy College, for his inspiration.

Finally, I will like to take this opportunity to thank the entire faculty and students of SUNY Maritime College, Mercy College, Long Island University, all my alma mater, for making me what I am today.

Chapter I

Mergers And Acquisitions Of The 1980s And The Mid-1990s

Introduction

Growth and expansion of assets, sales, and market share through acquisition is not a new corporate and business strategy, but it is a strategy that proliferated during the 1980s, lost steam during the early 1990s, and made a strong return in the mid-1990s. When one firm undertakes to acquire another, it generally embarks upon such action because the target firm complements the first firm's core business, the target has attractive assets that can be integrated into the first firm's portfolio, or the acquiring firm desires to put its competition out of business. Acquisitions can be friendly, in which it is anticipated that the target will remain in business, or hostile, in which it is anticipated that the target company will be sold off. When a firm is revealed to be a target of a takeover attempt, whether friendly or hostile, it draws to itself the attention of other firms or suitors, who may enter into a bidding war with the first firm.

One of the most bitter bidding wars in recent times(1994)was that between Viacom Incorporation and QVC Network Incorporation for control of Paramount Communications, the last major independent Hollywood studio, so as to "control programming in order to gain an edge for their distribution system as their competing technologies evolve[d]."[1] This bidding war, according to some Wall Street experts, was "one of the greatest takeover battles of the past 15 years."[2]

Before embarking upon an analytical study of the acquisition of Paramount communications by Viacom Incorporation, this book will attempt to present an overview of merger and acquisition activity in the U.S. economy in the 1980s and the mid-1990s, the period during which the Viacom and Paramount activity took place.

Background of the Acquisition Environment

Corporate mergers and acquisitions of the 1980s, as already mentioned, assumed historically high levels of activity in the U.S. economy.[3] Previous merger and acquisition activity, particularly in the 1960s, was primarily characterized by corporate diversification strategies, where the main objective was growth.[4] By contrast, hostile acquisitions, wherein the strategic objective frequently has minimal relevance to the primary business activity of acquiring firm, characterized most of the acquisition and merger activity of the 1980s.[5]

---

[1]Randall Smith, Johnnie L. Roberts, and Laura Landro. "Viacom Appears To Have Won Paramount War." *Wall Street Journal*, February 15, 1994, A3.

[2]Ibid.

[3]P. F. Drucker, "The Problem of Corporate Takeovers: What Is to Be Done?" *The Public Interest*, Winter 1986, 20.

[4]W. F. Glueck, *Business Policy and Strategic Management*, 4th ed. New York: McGraw-Hill Book Company, 1984), 274.

[5]"The M & A Watch: Is the This Any Way To Run A Company?" *Financial Executive*, March-April 1988, 1, 3-4.

To understand the fuel that powered acquisitions of the mid-1990s, the period of Viacom's takeover of Paramount, we must first consider(a)what impelled these activities in the 1980s, and(b)what effects the recession of early 1990 had on them. The key feature of the economic expansion of the 1980s, with respect to its role in driving up acquisitions, is that it was largely an upper-income phenomenon. This feature was in part a result of Reagan-era policies that included tax changes and labor policies. It was also a result of broader economic trends: the decline of relatively high-paid industrial jobs in favor of lower-paid service-sector jobs and international competition. As an illustration of the difference between the 1980s expansion and earlier expansions, the overall level of home ownership actually dropped during the 1980s, for the first time since 1930s.[6] The special nature of the 1980s expansion had a dual effect on the structure of the American economy. On the one hand, the incomes of the affluent increased sharply, which meant that many additional funds were available for investment. On the other hand, slow growth in middle-range incomes meant that relatively minimal additional funds were available for consumption of mid-range domestic goods and services. Growth in that type of consumption was, indeed, propelled largely by consumer borrowing.

The increase of Japanese and other foreign penetration of the American market had a similar effect. The Japanese policies have tended to reduce its domestic consumption and force savings, with the result that the increasing incomes of middle-income Japanese had much the same effect as an increase of upper-bracket incomes in its domestic economy: huge funds became available for lending and investment, while actual demand for new goods and services was only modest.

---

[6]Home Ownership Trends in the 1980s: U.S. Census Bureau Report, Series H121-90-2(Washington: U.S. Government Printing Office, 1990).

Overall, then, a large pool of funds was made available to investors and lenders, while there was relatively little call for investment in new plant and equipment in the U.S. economy. With little motivation to invest in the creation of *new* capital assets, such as plant and equipment, the available funds became channeled into an acquisition "bidding war" for assets.

On one level, this situation hiked the prices of real estate. On another level, the same "bidding war" led to corporate mergers and acquisitions of existing firms or assets. For tax purposes, and because debt, unlike equity, does not dilute voting control of companies, larger portions of the available money was lent and borrowed, rather than invested, in the narrow sense, as in equities. Debt propelled the corporate acquisitions of the 1980s.[7] These were, in a nutshell, the circumstances that led to the acquisitions of the 1980s. But by 1989, however, the flow of foreign funds into the American economy was beginning to taper off, in spite of some highly publicized acquisitions. The net capital inflow into the U.S. economy was $219 billion in 1988, shrinking gradually to only $215 billion in 1989.[8] Having now briefly examined the environment of the corporate takeovers during which the Viacom-Paramount transaction took place, we now turn to the entertainment and information industry in which Viacom and Paramount were operating.

---

[7]Karen Pennar, "This Dwarf Recession Might be a Giant," *Business Week*(October 15, 1990),30.

[8]"Foreign Investors Bought Fewer U.S. Assets Last Year," *Forbes*, 146(July 23, 1990), 356ff.

Analysis of the Entertainment and Information Industry

Entertainment

The bigger and financially stronger firms in the entertainment industry keep getting even stronger. The industry is somewhat immunized from exposure to general economic ups and downs.[9] In fact, its ability to withstand even the worst of economic downturn of 1929-30, the Great Depression, is well documented.[10]

Due to the fact that entertainment is cross-cultural, the business is inevitably worldwide in scope. With the U.S. being such a culturally diversified society among nations of the earth, it has considerable competitive advantage in the global stage. Being the most culturally diversified, the U.S. is most responsive aesthetically to cultures around the globe, perhaps more than a homogeneous society could be. As a historical writer on the subject noted:

> The cinema involves an aesthetic, a technology, an economy and an audience; and all four of these elements will condition what moving images appear upon the screen at any particular place and in any particular period. The aesthetic, technology, economy and audience which resulted, in 1895, in motion pictures as we now know them and which shaped the early years of the medium, have their origins long before the Lumières and the Salon Indien.[11]

---

[9]Ben Sharav, "Entertainment Industry," *Value Line Investment Survey*, May 30, 1997, 1778.

[10]David Robinson, *The History of World Cinema*, Revised and Updated.(New York: Stein and Day, 1981), 179.

[11]David Robinson, *The History of World Cinema*, Revised and Updated.(New York: Stein and Day, 1981), 1.

The technological and economic temper of the U.S., especially right after World War I, coupled with its high cultural diversity mentioned earlier, well positioned the U.S. to overwhelmingly dominate the entertainment industry in the global arena. Today, the special appeal of American culture, as depicted in films, is very much on the ascendancy. For example, as an industry analyst pointed out:

> while in the U.S., "foreign" films tend to find audiences only in art houses catering to intellectuals, the masses across the globe watch Hollywood movies. This has created growth opportunities for American entertainment companies to distribute movies and music and sell related products.[12]

The industry belongs to the so-called "intellectual property" business. To come out with the underlying "product," such as a screenplay or a song, requires only creativity. This means that, it does not require large fixed assets that go into heavy manufacturing industries like automobiles. For this reason, it may appear that small firms could thrive economically in the industry. Interestingly, the reverse is the case for many reasons, including distribution. The bigger firms are able to overwhelm the market with a steady array of products, securing advantageous positions within the distribution network. Another reason pertains to the growing demand on the part of the public or the audience for more elaborate and spectacular entertainment product. For example, as Ben Sharav, an industry analyst noted, producing a movie with name stars and big special effects could easily run into $50 million. These reasons make big firms such as Walt Disney and Time Warner dominant in the industry.[13]

The quest for synergy, that is, fusing the resources and expertise of two companies with an expectation that each will complement the other,

---

[12]Ben Sharav, "Entertainment Industry," Value Line Investment Survey, May 30, 1997, 1778.

[13]Ibid.

which will in turn lead to a value and competitive power for the combined firm which are greater than the combined values and competitive power of the two separate companies, is yet another reason for acquisitions. A major movie, for example, requires a huge initial capital outlay to produce. But once produced, it can easily be duplicated and adapted to different media formats at a relatively cheap cost. Disney and Time Warner create movies for theatrical release and also package them in videocassette format for sale and rental. Disney acquired the ABC TV network, gaining an additional outlet. Similarly, Time Warner acquired Turner Broadcasting Systems in 1996, in addition to its prior ownership of Cable TV systems and pay-per-view networks on which it shows movies, thus roping in additional profit. The quest for synergies in the industry go well beyond presenting the products in different formats. In fact, among the most essential assets of entertainment firms are their trademark characters and titles, which can constitute the basis of derivative products that stretch across various media. For example, Disney and Time Warner generate immense profits by making use of successful movies through franchises which include music, theme park attractions, books, and memorabilia.[14]

This advantage may be one of the reasons, as we shall see later in this book, why Paramount offered such a synergistic allure for Viacom. Paramount had, just prior to its acquisition by Viacom, acquired Macmillan Publishing Company which had an excellent distribution network, for $553 million in cash, consummated on February 28, 1994.[15]

---

[14]Ben Sharav, "Entertainment Industry," *Value Line Investment Survey*, May 30, 1997, 1778.

[15]U.S. *Mergers & Acquisitions* magazine, vol. 29/number 1, July/August 1994, 76.

Information

The second meaning of the word "information" in Webster's ency-clopedic dictionary is "any knowledge gained through communication, research, instruction." In light of this definition, the distinction between the words "entertainment" and "information" is blurred. The entertainment industry cannot really be divorced from the information industry, for they share the common ground of passing along knowledge through communication as a way of instructing to help mold society, or the audience's behavior. For this reason industry analysts almost always group them under the title "entertainment & information." Granted this linkage, analysis of the entertainment industry equally holds true for the information industry. For example, Elizabeth Comte, an industry analyst, writes about the "entertainment & information" industry as comprising "movie companies, television networks, and publishers." Going beyond this narrow definition of information could throw us off track. For example, we might find ourselves dealing with the so-called computer information systems, which is outside the scope of this paper.

Financial Strength of the Industry

For the past five years, beginning in 1993 and ending in 1997, a period in which the Viacom-Paramount transaction took place, the industry's composite statistics showed it about maintained its growth and profitability, except for 1994 when there was a slight slump. In the years 1993 through 1997, operating margins were 17.9%, 16.9%, 18.1%, 18.4%, and 18.2% respectively.[16] These figures mean that for each dol-lar of the respective year's sales, those figures, translated as cents, remained as profit from operations.

---

[16]"Composite Statistics: Entertainment Industry." Value Line Investment Survey, May 30, 1997, 1778.

Chapter II

Analysis Of Paramount Communications And Viacom Incorporation At The Time Of The Transaction

Paramount Communications

Historical Background

Paramount Communications, at the time of its acquisition by Viacom Incorporation, was a media giant already. It maintained operations in the entertainment and publishing industries. Its areas of operation included the production of motion pictures, production of television programs, cable and broadcast television, prerecorded home videocassette production and distribution, professional sports and other events, and educational and consumer publishing. Its operating units in entertainment included Madison Square Garden, New York Knicks Basketball Club, New York Rangers Hockey Club, Paramount Pictures, and the USA cable network(a joint venture). The publishing operating unit included Simon & Schuster, Prentice Hall, Webster's New World Dictionaries, Pocket Books, and just prior to its acquisition by Viacom, it had acquired Macmillan Publishing as mentioned earlier.[1]

The company had a long history, having been the first Hollywood studio started in 1912 by Adolph Zukor. It became Paramount Pictures after merging with Famous Players-Lasky, a studio formed by Jesse Lasky, Samuel Goldwyn(né Goldfish), and Cecil B. DeMille. During the 1940s the government forced Paramount to spin off its theater holdings. Movie attendance slipped as TV grew, and in 1966 Gulf & Western purchased the struggling Paramount Pictures. Gulf & Western began in 1956 when Charles G. Bludhorn bought Michigan Plating and Stamping(Studebaker rear bumpers). A couple of years later, he merged his company with Beard and Stone Electric, and in 1959 adopted the name Gulf & Western Industries. The company acquired numerous diverse firms.[2] When Bludhorn died in 1983, his successor, Martin Davis who was in control of Paramount at the time of its acquisition by Viacom, sold off 65 of the more than 100 companies owned by Gulf & Western. Davis chose to focus on the entertainment and publishing industries, and in 1989 the company was renamed Paramount Communications.[3]

---

[1] Peggy Kneffel Daniels, and Susan E. Edgar, Eds., *Job Seeker's Guide.* 2nd Ed., Vol. 3, The Northeast(Detroit: Gale Research International Ltd., 1995), 433.

[2] Patrick J. Spain, and James R. Talbot, Eds., *Hoover's Handbook of American Business: Profilesof Major U.S. Companies.*(Austin, TX: The Reference Press, 1995), 1506.

[3] Peggy Kneffel Daniels, and Susan E. Edgar, Eds., Job Seeker's Guide. 2nd Ed., Vol. 3, The Northeast(Detroit: Gale Research International Ltd., 1995), 433.

Financial Condition

In 1933, Paramount ranked 219th on the "Forbes 500: America's Largest Firms."[4] Revenues for the firm had steadily risen over the last eight years at the time of its acquisition, with annual growth of 14 percent for the last five of the eight years Its earnings had been less predictable, with earnings posting an annual rate of change of–5 percent for that last five years.[5] At year end 1992, improved results at Paramount Communications' motion pictures unit and publishing businesses led to a 22 percent increase in fourth-quarter profit, to $101.4 million from $83.3 million.[6]

Investors and industry analysts were encouraged by the rise in Paramount's stock price on January 21, 1993. The stock rose 31/2 to 46 1/8, with some saying the company was one of the best ways to play the growing demand for "software" in the media and communications businesses.[7] However, the company's revenues had been increasing, but its profit picture had been mixed.[8]

Paramount posted a 95 percent plunge in fiscal first-quarter of 1994 earnings to $900,000 from $18.4 million a year earlier. Revenue fell to $943.7 million from $1.1 billion. The company cited weakness in feature films and seasonal losses in publishing as the reasons for this

---

[4]Ibid.

[5]Marc Gerstein, "Paramount Communications," *Value Line Investment Survey,* March 4, 1994, 1767.

[6]Johnnie L. Roberts, "Paramount Net Increased 22% in Fiscal 4th Period," *Wall Street Journal,* 13 January 1993, A5, Col. 1.

[7]Roberts, "Paramount's 3½ Point Stock Jump Spotlights Brighter Outlook, *Wall Street Journal,* 22 January 1993, C2, Col. 3.

[8]Gerstein, "Paramount," 1767.

plunge.[9] Revenues and net income for 1992 were $4.2 billion and $261.4 million respectively, with a work force of 12,000.[10]

Viacom Incorporation

Historical Background

Incorporated in Delaware on November 10, 1986, Viacom Incorporation was formed by CBS in 1970, after the Federal Communications Commission ruled that TV networks could not own cable systems and TV stations in the same market. Viacom took over CBS's program syndication division. In the early part of the 1970s, Viacom purchased cable systems in five states. In 1978, the company formed "Showtime," a subscription TV service, with Teleprompter, becoming complete owner in 1982. As one of the world's largest media firms, Viacom is both the medium and the message. Prior to its 1994 acquisition of Paramount, the company's major business lines were cable television networks, including MTV, "Nickelodeon," and "Showtime." A major force in TV, it maintains ownership of such cable channels as MTV, VH-1, "Nickelodeon/Nick at Nite," pay movie channels(Showtime, the Movie Channel, and Flix), and Sci-Fi Channel, and the All News Channel. It is a major producer of leading TV shows("Entertainment Tonight" and "Frasier," among others); a syndicator of popular TV programs(the "Star Trek" series, "Cheers," and "Taxi"); a major movie producer("Forest Gump"); a leading book publisher(Simon & Schuster); and the world's

---

[9]Johnnie L. Roberts, "Paramount Communications Earnings Plummeted 95% in Fiscal 1st Quarter," Wall Street Journal, 11 March 1993, B9, Col. 4.

[10]Geraldine Fabrikant, "Paramount-Viacom Talks Heat Up," New York Times, 11 September 1993. L39.

top video and music retailer(Blockbuster Video and Blockbuster Music). The diversified entertainment giant company also owns several radio and TV stations, and presides over a library of TV programs and feature films. It further operates regional theme parks, and owns movie theaters in the U.S., Europe, and Canada. In 1983, Viacom and Warner/Amex combined "Showtime" with "The Movie Channel" to form "Showtime Networks." American Express left the Warner/Amex joint venture in 1986, and Viacom purchased Warner's share of Showtime Networks and MTV Networks, including cable's first all-music video channel. The company also began the production of series for network TV and purchased a St. Louis TV station.

In 1987, Viacom's current chairman, Mr. Sumner Redstone, owner of National Amusements, a movie theater chain, purchased 83 percent of Viacom for $3.4 billion, following a bidding war against Carl Icahn and a Viacom management group. It tried unsuccessfully to acquire Orion Pictures in 1988.[11]

Financial Condition

In 1992, Viacom's television segment contributed 29 percent of the company's operating profits, and was serving approximately one million subscribers. Its five broadcasting network affiliate stations(which included three NBC stations and two CBS stations), contributed 8 percent of the 1992 operating profits. The company's network segment, which operates several cable television channels, including Nickelodeon, Showtime, The Movie Channel, MTV, and VH-1, mentioned earlier, contributed 49 percent of the 1992 operating profits. Its entertainment segment which

---

[11]Patrick J. Spain, and James R. Talbot, Eds., *Hoover's Handbook of American Business: Profiles of Major U.S. Companies*(Austin, TX: The Reference Press, 1995), 1506.

distributes television programs, including "The Cosby Show," "A Different World," and "Roseanne" contributed 14 percent of 1992's operating profits. Similar to Paramount Communications, Viacom's revenues had increased since 1988 to the time of acquiring Paramount. Also similar to Paramount, Viacom's profit picture had been mixed, posting losses in four of the past six years as at March 1994.[12] Viacom's 1992 revenues and net income were $1.9 billion and $66 million respectively. Its number of employees were 4,700, less than one-half that of Paramount.[13] The company was, therefore, going to swallow a fish more than twice its size, both in terms of revenue and labor force.

Basis For The Transaction

One study identified two different types of synergy which may be associated with mergers. These synergy kinds are "operational" synergy and "financial" synergy.[14] The study discovered that financial synergy typically creates greater value than does operational synergy. An operational synergy involves the *integration* of the two combining firms after the acquisition has been consummated. A good example of this kind of synergy was Chemical Bank-Manufacturers Hanover. Financial synergy, on the other hand, is one where the merged firms will not be operated

---

[12]Marc Gerstein, "Viacom, Inc.," *Value Line Investment Survey*, March 25, 1994, 386.

[13]Geraldine Fabrinkant, "Paramount-Viacom Talks Heat Up," *New York Times*, September 11, 1993, L39.

[14]S. Chatterjeu, "Types of Synergy and Economic Value: The Impact of Acquisitions on Merging and Rival Firms," *Strategic Management Journal*, 7(1986): 119-139.

as a single unit as in operational synergy, and from which no significant operating economies are anticipated.[15]

Sensible motives for acquisitions and mergers are found when the positions of each company involved in the action will be improved. Among these sensible motives are included(1)capital requirements by an acquired company,(2)the meshing of distribution systems,(3)complementing customer bases, and(4)similar reasons. Frequently, one company will undertake to acquire another company with either low or no net earnings, or possibly with tax credits. Under such cases, the acquiring company may be able to decrease its own federal income tax liability. When an acquiring company is able to decrease its federal income tax liability through acquisition or merger, it in effect increases its net worth.[16] But as we noted earlier, Paramount's net income of $261.4 million almost quadrupled Viacom's $66 million in 1992. This section, therefore, attempts to find the "sensible motives" in this acquisition. Of course, as noted by the authors, Weston and Brigham, cited earlier, mergers may actually combine both financial and operational synergies. There were both operational and financial rationale for the vertical integration of Viacom and Paramount.

The two companies did not overlap significantly in their operating businesses, with the exception of some TV stations and cable services. A merger would create a vertically integrated company that controlled both the production and distribution of entertainment programming. The film studio Paramount Pictures unit of Paramount Communications, for example, could produce films for Viacom's Showtime Movie Channel that could be distributed on Viacom's cable

---

[15]J. Fred Weston, and Eugene F. Brigham, *Essentials of Managerial Finance*, 10th Ed.(New York: The Dryden Press, 1993), 839.

[16]E. F. Brigham, *Financial Management*, 4th Ed.(Hinsdale, Illinois: The Dryden Press, 1985), 704-705.

systems.[17] Thus, this merger offered synergistic competitive advantage for the combining firms. Additionally, a merged:

> Paramount-Viacom company would have a market capital-ization of roughly $17 billion with about $2.4 billion in debt. That would put the company in a stronger financial position than Time Warner [a major competitor,] which had a market capitalization of $25 billion but some $11 bil-lion of debt.[18]

Thus, from both operational standpoint and financial standpoint, there were greater similarity and possibly greater synergy between Paramount and Viacom, both of which were engaged in the production and distribution of broadcast and filmed products. The allure for Paramount was even greater in the light of the fact that it had just acquired Macmillan Publishing, with its excellent distribution system.

---

[17]Geraldine Fabrikant, "Paramount-Viacom Talks Heat Up," *New York Times,* September 11,1993, L39.

[18]Ibid.

Chapter III

The Acquisition Process And The Emergence Of Rival Bidder For Control Of Paramount

Techniques Of Corporate Acquisitions

There are two main scenarios of the corporate takeover process. One is the "multistep acquisition" technique, and the other is the "traditional single step merger" technique.[1]

Multistep Acquisition Technique

The multistep process, sometimes called the "three-piece suitor," passes through three sequential phases, hence its name. The first step is the "block stock purchase" whereby the acquiring firm negotiates the

---

[1]James C. Freund, and Richard L. Easton, "The Three-Piece Suitor: An Alternative Approach to Negotiated Corporate Acquisitions," The *Thirteenth Forum on Negotiating Corporate Acquisitions. Public & Private,*(New York: Law Journal Seminars-Press, 1989), 25-36.

buying of a large block of stock of the target firm, usually for cash, from a controlling stockholder or from a large non-institutional investor. Ideally, the transacting companies allow for a simultaneous signing and closing of the agreement, with the chief collateral provision in the agreement being the acquirer's undertaking to make a cash offer to all other stockholders of the target firm. A press release(see sample figure 3.1)is issued, following the signing of the agreement, announcing that the bidder has acquired the block of stock and has undertaken to make a tender offer on comparable terms to all other stockholders of the target firm.

Ideally, this is a "friendly" tender offer which simply means that the target firm's management is being cooperative in the transaction. There are situations in which it may be hostile tender offer, that is, the target firm's management is actively opposed to the takeover. For example, Paramount's management were opposed to the rival bidder, QVC Network Incorporation, taking over Paramount, as we shall see later in this chapter. But in the ideal case, the acquirer, through this press release, is asking stockholders of the target firm to submit or "tender" their shares in exchange for the price it is paying for the controlling stockholder, or the large non-institutional investor.

The second phase of this technique is the "tender offer," or the "friendly" tender offer itself. It is a direct appeal to the target firm's stockholders, for any or all of their shares, at the same price as was paid for the block, backed by the target firm's management's recommendation. Optimally, the target firm's board of directors should recommend the acceptance of the offer to its stockholders, or at least refrain from opposing it, if the timing of the acquisition is to be significantly expedited. For example, the target firm's board of directors may cooperate by providing a list of their stockholders' mailing addresses to be informed about the offer.

Figure 3.1 American Home Products press release.

AMERICAN HOME PRODUCTS CORPORATION
FIVE GIRALDA FARMS, MADISON, NEW JERSEY 07940,(201)660-5000

EXECUTIVE OFFICES

FOR IMMEDIATE RELEASE:

Investor Contact:
John R. Considina
(201)660-6429

Media Contact:
Louis V. Cafiero
(201)660-5013

AMERICAN HOME PRODUCTS TO COMMENCE CASH TENDER
OFFER FOR AMERICAN CYANAMID AT $95 PER SHARE

Madison, N.J., August 9, 1994—American Home Products Corporation (NYSE:AHP)announced today that its Board of Directors has formally approved the Company's previously announced offer to purchase American Cyanamid Company for $95 per share in cash. In furtherance of this offer, the Board authorized the commencement of a cash tender offer for all of the outstanding stock of American Cyanamid at that price, subject to customary conditions for an offer of this nature.

John R. Stafford, Chairman, President and Chief Executive Officer of American Home Products, stated that "although we are starting our tender offer, we are confident that American Cyanamid's Board of Directors will recognize the inherent value of our offer to their stockholders, and we hope they will quickly accept our invitation to begin meaningful discussions for a negotiated transaction."

American Home Products also announced that it was commencing litigation designed to eliminate the applicability to its offer of certain of American Cyanamid's anti-takeover and other defensive provisions. In addition, American Home Products stated that it intends to solicit other American Cyanamid stockholders to join it in calling for a special stockholders meeting to act on matters relating to the American Home Products offer.

Source: Gaughan Patrick A., *Mergers, Acquisitions and Corporate Restructurings,*(New York: John Wiley & Sons, Inc., 1996)

The third step is the cash takeover, and it results when the acquirer, having become successful in acquiring majority of the target's stocks through its tender offer, casts the stockholders' majority vote in its own favor. At this point, the target's remaining stockholders who turned down the tender offer are involuntarily eliminated, and receive cash payment in return for their shares. They do, retain what is called "stock appraisal rights" to ensure they receive fair price for their shares. The target is now acquired.

The major advantage of this multistep process centers on speed. Corporate acquisition is a raid of one company by another, and the battle-tested art of speed and timing in the military equally holds true in this case. This process substantially diminishes the chances of a competing bidder's intervention and freezes out competition because, just as potential rival bidders find out about the deal, the acquirer has already locked up a huge chunk of the target's stock and is about to initiate its tender offer. Even though the acquirer does not yet own the target, any competitor to the bidding war is not beginning from a point of equality. Another advantage of this process, unlike the traditional single step acquisition, which we will examine shortly, is that a two-thirds vote of the target's outstanding shares is not required for the deal's approval, which may not be forthcoming. Through this process, with its substantial block purchase and successful tender offer, the acquirer already owns enough voting powers to approve the acquisition without any resort to outside votes.

Its major drawback is the uncertainty that surrounds the success of the tender offer. With an insufficient initial block stock purchase, the acquirer may still lack working control over the target firm. If the tender offer proves to be unsuccessful, the acquirer could find itself left with a large investment that it has bought at a premium, and which the market may not support, yet lacking control of the target.

Traditional Single Step Merger Technique

This approach begins with a preliminary negotiations between the transacting parties. Each party tests the pulse of the other, with the objective of finding a mutually satisfactory valuation of the target firm. The so-called "agreement in principle" on the transaction is arrived at if there is a mutually agreed upon price, and perhaps job security for the target's management. The agreement in principle may take the form of oral agreement, or the form of the so-called "letter of intent," stating the parties' intention to merge at a specific price. But it is subject to further negotiation and execution of a "definitive acquisition agreement," the target's board of directors, and stockholders' approval, permission of antitrust regulators, and the concurrence of major creditors. This essentially means that the agreement in principle is not binding until the signing and approval of the "definitive acquisition agreement."

The agreement in principle, however, demonstrates the seriousness of the deal to the parties, and a press release is issued, describing the basic terms of the deal. Nothing prevents other rival bidders interested in the target from intervening. Notice how this press release is different from that of the multistep approach, which announces that the acquirer has already bought a large chunk of stock of the target firm, and that it is initializing a tender offer for the remaining stock.

At this point under the single-step approach, intense, full-scale, and time-consuming financial investigation commences from both antitrust regulators and the transacting parties. In contrast with the multistep approach, in which the acquirer may well be in possession of a substantial majority of the target firm's shares, enough to perhaps discourage rival intervention, by the time the negotiating parties in the single-step approach get around to signing and closing a definitive acquisition agreement, the acquirer still owns nothing of the target, short of contractual agreement.

The major advantage of this approach is that because it undergoes thorough scrutiny, verification, and time-consuming investigation, it is less prone to litigation than the multistep approach. Also, because it is so time consuming, it offers the advantage that by the time the acquirer lays down its money on the line, it is fully certain of what it is getting in return. The risks embedded in ignorance of the facts about the target are substantially reduced.

Its major disadvantage is that being so time consuming, and the acquirer having no substantial possession in the shares of the target, it encourages rival bidders' intervention, as was the case of the Paramount-Viacom transaction which we shall shortly examine.

In addition, its time-consuming nature may permit a so-called "white knight," that is, a company that is loaded with money and is more acceptable to the target firm's management, to jump on the scene to the rescue of the target firm, and thus prevent the first acquirer from closing a deal.[2]

The Acquisition Process of Paramount by Viacom and the Bidding War

Preliminary Negotiations and Press Release

It is quite obvious from the examination of the two main takeover scenarios that Paramount and Viacom chose the traditional single-step

---

[2]James C. Freund, and Richard L. Easton, "The Three-Piece Suitor: An Alternative Approach to Negotiated Corporate Acquisitions," *The Thirteenth Forum on Negotiating Corporate Acquisitions. Public & Private,*(New York: Law Journal Seminars-Press, 1989), 25-36.

merger approach. Perhaps, the first public revelation of the Paramount-Viacom deal was September 9, 1993, when the Wall Street Journal reported that, "Paramount Communications Inc. is expected to discuss a possible merger with Viacom Inc. at a regularly scheduled meeting of Paramount directors today."[3] Viacom's chairman, Sumner Redstone, summed up his company's management philosophy when he remarked that, "we're always on the lookout for new opportunities [to grow]."[4] In fact, as several executives close to the deal had noted, "the companies' chairmen-Sumner Redstone at Viacom and Martin S. Davis at Paramount-have held on-again off-again talks for several years, and added that this latest round could fall apart at the last minute. But one executive close to the proposed deal said talks had proceeded to the point that he felt fairly certain the merger would occur."[5] This activity represented the preliminary discussions under the traditional single step approach. Each party was testing the pulse of the other, with the aim of arriving at a mutually satisfactory valuation of Paramount, and perhaps the role that Paramount's management would play after the acquisition, that is, job security.

Following the press report about the impending Paramount-Viacom negotiation, on September 12, 1993, Paramount Communications announced a $69.14-a-share, $8.2 billion merger with Viacom Incorporation.[6]

---

[3]Staff Reporter, "Paramount Board May Act On Possible Viacom Deal," Wall Street Journal, September 9, 1993, B12, col.1.

[4]Elizabeth Comte, "Giving viewers a Choice," Forbes, January 4, 1993, 142.

[5]Geraldine Fabrikant, "Paramount-Viacom Talks Heat Up," New York Times, September 11, 1993, L37.

[6]Randall Smith, "Wall Street's Final Analysis: Might Made Right," Wall Street Journal February 16, 1994, B1.

QVC Network Incorporation Jumps On The Scene

At about the same time that Paramount announced its intended merger with Viacom, the rumor mill began swirling around,

> that a bid for Paramount might come from a group of investors led by John C. Malone, chief executive of the cable giant Tele-Communications Inc. [TCI], and Barry Diller, head of the cable shopping Network QVC which is controlled by Mr. Malone[7]

QVC Network, Inc. marketed and sold consumer products and services through a televised shopping channel which broadcasted 24 hours a day, 7 days a week to approximately 50 million cable subscribers and viewers with satellite dishes. The company's products included jewelry, collectibles, electronics, and toys. It acquired CVN Companies in October 1989 making it the largest televised shopping service. As with the other companies involved in the acquisition-Viacom and Paramount-QVC had increases in revenues since its inception in 1986 with average annual increases of 43.5 percent over the past five years. Also similar to the other companies involved in the acquisition, its profit picture had been less favorable, with losses posted in 1986, 1987, and 1990. The company's net profit margin had been increasing to a high of 6.5 percent in 1993.[8]

As noted earlier(see chapter II), there was greater similarity and possibly greater synergy between Paramount and Viacom, both of which are involved in the production and distribution of broadcast and filmed

---

[7]Fabrikant, New York Times, September 11, 1993, L37.

[8]Timothy F. Tucker, "QVC Network," Value Line Investment Survey, February 25, 1994, 1705.

product.QVC does not appear at first to be a good suitor as a parent of Paramount until one realizes that Barry Diller, the head of QVC at the time of the acquisition, formerly headed Paramount when it was owned by Gulf & Western. It was Diller who brought into Paramount Michael Eisner and Jeffrey Katzenberg(who at the time of the acquisition had left and were chairmen of the Waltz Disney Company and Waltz Disney Studios chief, respectively), who were generally credited with helping to turn Paramount around.[9]

In addition to the personal connection between Diller and Paramount, the QVC bid for Paramount made sense on business terms. While not as closely related as Viacom and Paramount, QVC's acquisition of Paramount would have provided it with a strong presence in the production sector, and all three companies-Paramount, Viacom, and QVC-were members of the communications industry.

About one week after Paramount announced its friendly deal with Viacom, the rumors were confirmed. On September 20, 1993, QVC Network , after obtaining $1 billion from Comcast Corporation, Liberty Media(TCI's former programming subsidiary), nd John Malone's Tele-Communications Incorporation among others, upped the stakes to an $80-a-share, $9.5 billion hostile bid for Paramount. Viacom responded on September 24, 1993, by suggesting that Tele-Communications' chief, John Malone, was trying to control every aspect of the cable industry, and that a movie channel backed by Liberty allies would launch a number of movie channels that would compete directly against Viacom's, and thus monopolize the cable TV business. Liberty eventually backed out of the Paramount war when it agreed to be purchased by the Bell Atlantic regional phone company.[10]

---

[9]James Bates, "Paramount Deal," Los Angeles Times, February 16, 1994, A16.

[10]Randall Smith, "Wall Street's Final Analysis: Might Made Right," Wall Street Journal, February 16, 1994, B1.

With Liberty out of the running, both Viacom and QVC sought new partners in order to strengthen their balance sheets to raise their Paramount bid. It marked the first appearance of huge alliances between companies in different sectors of the media business, particularly regional Bell operating companies.[11] Viacom allied itself with Nynex, a regional phone company, and Blockbuster Entertainment Corporation. Viacom's Redstone put together an $8.4 billion merger with Blockbuster, thus giving Viacom access to Blockbuster's strong cash flow and nearly debt-free balance sheet,[12] and giving "Viacom's bid a psychological solidity,"[13] noted Lisbeth Barron, an industry expert. According to Randall Smith,

> Because he [Viacom's chairman, Mr. Sumner Redstone] held 85% of voting control due to his ownership of supervoting Viacom Class A shares, Mr. Redstone was able to negotiate a deal in which he would issue stock to acquire Blockbuster[14]

QVC's Diller, on his part, sought out yet another regional phone company, BellSouth, and Cox Enterprises, a cable and newspaper company.[15]

---

[11] Ibid.
[12] Ibid.
[13] Ibid.
[14] Ibid.
[15] Ibid.

Chapter IV

The Financial And Non-Financial Considerations Apparent In The Paramount-Viacom Action

Rationale Behind Acquisitions

To enhance our comprehension of the financial and non-financial considerations that were apparent in the Paramount-Viacom deal, this chapter will first present the general motives that drive corporate acquisitions. Unquestionably, mergers and acquisitions are undertaken by executives with certain objectives in mind. Whatever these reasons may be, they may be defined in terms of the acquirer's corporate and business strategy objectives. There are essentially two possible motives for companies to undertake acquisitions. One is the so-called "neo-classical profit maximization model," and the other is the "managerial utility model."[1]

---

[1] P.S. Sudarsanam, *The Essence of Mergers and Acquisitions*,(Cornwall, U.K.: Prentice Hall, 1995), 13-16.

Under the neo-classical profit maximization motive, managers formulate strategies and acquisition decisions to further the profit interest of the shareholders. Here, the shareholders' interest is of utmost importance, subordinating managerial interests. For example, all companies exist to make profit for their owners, and this profit maximization is achieved when the added value created by the acquisition excels the cost of the acquisition.

The other motive, the managerial utility perspective, stems from management's self-interest. For example, managers may acquire another company(1)to avoid becoming a target firm themselves(job security),(2)to go after external growth in the size of their company, since their remuneration, perquisites, status, and power are a function of company size(empire-building syndrome),(3)to diversify risk and diminish the costs of financial distress and bankruptcy(job security), and(4)to deploy their currently underutilized but expensive managerial talents and skills, so that they can lease these talents to the acquired firm, and consult later as needed in order to trim down on payroll costs(self-fulfilment motive).[2] Executive compensation may increase as a consequence of increase in company size, which is manifested as assets or sales of the company. Where managers compensation is directly related to sales growth , they may pursue growth through acquisitions.

These two possible motives, the neo-classical profit maximization motive and the managerial utility motive, distill into five working rationales for corporate acquisitions. These are(1)Synergy,(2)Tax Considerations,(3)Purchase of Assets below their Replacement Costs,(4)Diversification, and(5)Maintaining Control.[3] They are now discussed in turn.

2P.S. Sudarsanam, *The Essence of Mergers and Acquisitions,*(Cornwall, U.K.: Prentice Hall, 1995), 13-16.

3J. Fred Weston, and Eugene F. Brigham, *Essentials of Managerial Finance*, 10th Ed.(New York: The Dryden Press, 1993), 831-833.

1. Synergy

The basic rationale for mergers and acquisitions is to increase the value of the combined firms. For example, if Paramount is acquired by Viacom, and the two merged firm's value surpasses that of Viacom and Paramount taken separately, then synergy is said to exist. In other words, the whole is greater than the sum of the parts.[4]

2. Tax Considerations

Tax motives also play a part in mergers and acquisitions. For example, a company making huge profits and falling within the highest corporate tax bracket may acquire a firm with huge accumulated tax losses, then utilize those losses to shelter its own income. This benefit, however, could be challenged by the IRS if it can be proven(which is difficult due to the several factors that may be inherent in a given acquisition)that tax considerations were the only and overriding motives. In the same vein, a firm experiencing heavy losses could acquire a company making high profits. Also, tax considerations may be involved in mergers and acquisitions as a vehicle for utilizing excess cash, which if unused, may open it up as a target of acquisition itself. For example, a company that has ran out of internal opportunities for investment in relation to its cash flows will have excess cash, and its options for disposal of this excess cash are(1)to pay extra dividends to shareholders,(2)to invest it in marketable securities,(3)to repurchase its own stock, or(4)to buy another company.

If it opts for paying extra dividends, its stockholders will have to pay taxes on the distribution. Marketable securities such as Treasury bills have lower rate of return than required by stockholders. A stock repurchase might lead to a capital gain for the remaining stockholders, but could have a drawback if the company had to pay a high price to acquire the stock, and if the repurchase was purposely to avoid paying dividends, it

---

[4]Ibid.

might be challenged by the IRS. But utilizing excess cash to acquire another company has no instant tax consequences for either the acquirer or its stockholder. Thus, tax considerations may influence the number of acquisitions to be undertaken.[5]

3. Purchase of Assets below Their Replacement Cost
A company may also undertake an acquisition because the replacement value of its assets is substantially in excess of its market value. For example, Chevron acquired Gulf Oil, a reserve, more cheaply than by exploratory drilling.[6]

4. Diversification
Executives frequently cite diversification to stabilize their company's earnings and reduce corporate risk as a reason for acquisitions.[7] In other words the two firms belong to the same industry but as one is peaking in sales in the business cycle, the other may be troughing. In such case, a merger may offset the non-synchronized income streams of the two companies, averaging them out for the common good.

5. Maintaining Control
As mentioned earlier in the preface to this paper, the human toll of mergers and acquisitions can be quite traumatic. Managers of the acquired companies generally lose their jobs, or their autonomy. This impact is especially noted in hostile takeovers. Hence, managers look for ways to avoid becoming takeover targets and remain in control. For example, when Enron Corporation became a target for acquisition, it

---

[5] J. Fred Weston, and Eugene F. Brigham, *Essentials of Managerial Finance*, 10th Ed.(New York: The Dryden Press, 1993), 831-833.

[6] Ibid.

[7] Ibid.

negotiated to purchase Houston Natural Gas Company, paying primarily with debt. This acquisition made Enron a much larger company and difficult to "digest." Coupled with the much higher debt level as a consequence of its acquisition of Houston, the deal rendered Enron less attractive for any potential acquirer to utilize debt to purchase it. Enron's executives invariable advanced the argument of synergistic benefits, and not their job security, as the reason for the acquisition. But several acquisitions have been undertaken more for the benefit of the firm's management than for stockholders.[8]

The Financial and Non-Financial Considerations Inherent in the Paramount-Viacom Deal

The financial and non-financial considerations that became apparent in the Viacom takeover of Paramount ran the whole gamut from talks of synergy, boost in market capitalization, grand corporate alliances, clashing of egos, to culminating in legal actions, as we noted earlier. The four major players were Mr. Sumner Redstone, Viacom chairman, Mr. Martin Davis, Paramount chief executive, Mr. Barry Diller, QVC chairman, and Mr. Wayne Huizenga, Blockbuster chairman. The contention led to huge corporate alliances which some investment bankers believed,

"such alliances are [were] well suited to the fast evolving technologies of the media business, where companies with different delivery mechanisms,

---

[8]J. Fred Weston, and Eugene F. Brigham, *Essentials of Managerial Finance*, 10th ed.(New York: The Dryden Press, 1993), 831-833.

from cable TV to telecomunications, may join forces to gain a critical asset like the Paramount movie studio that fills [filled] their need for programming."[9]

Financial Considerations

The empire-building syndrome for growth through external acquisitions, with its attendant remuneration, perquisites, status, and power which are a function of company size discussed earlier, undoubtedly was a factor in the Paramount-Viacom action, as hinted by Viacom chairman, Mr. Redstone, in his remark that his company was on the lookout for opportunities to expand.[10] Mr. Davis , Paramount CEO was certainly happy with the merger because it was going to increase his own wealth and the strength of Paramount as a media giant. This was true in spite of the fact that Mr. Redstone was going to be in effective control. Yet history had shown that Mr. Redstone tended to rely on subordinates to run his firms, as he was doing with Mr. Frank Biondi Jr. for Viacom. Redstone wanted to be a major force in entertainment and to expand his holding to the huge size that would be possible under the merger.[11]

Also, as previously noted(see chapter II), a combination of Paramount and Viacom was going to result in a market capitalization of about $17 billion with only $2.4 billion in debt. The merger would place the combined company in a stronger financial position than its major competitor, Time Warner, which had a market capitalization of $25 billion but a high debt of $11 billion, in an industry where size and

---

[9]Randall Smith, "Wall Street's Final Analysis: Might Made Right," *Wall Street Journal*, February 16, 1994, B1.

[10]Elizabeth Comte, "Giving Viewers a Choice," *Forbes*, January 4, 1993, 142.

[11]Laura Landro, "Grit Bolsters Viacom Chief in Takeover Bid," *Wall Street Journal*, November 16, 1993, B1, B16.

financial strength are key factors in competitive advantage.[12] So there would be financial synergy in this merger.

Ample evidence existed too that operational synergy was also a consideration since Paramount and Viacom were both engaged in producing and distributing broadcast and filmed products.

The recent acquisition of Macmillan Publishing and its superb distribution network, made Paramount even more alluring for Viacom. As noted earlier, the film studio Paramount Pictures, for example, could produce films for Viacom's Showtime Movie Channel that could be distributed on Viacom's systems.[13]

Moreover, Paramount had a debt of only $700 million, compared with Viacom's $2.4 billion, leaving Paramount in a position to pay down some of Viacom's debt.[14] As noted by a *Wall Street Journal* staff reporter, "…the company [Paramount] is [was] fat with trophy assets waiting to be managed better. Its $1.2 billion in cash and relatively low debt make [made] it a stellar candidate to be acquired-or to mount a takeover of its own."[15]

Non-financial Considerations

Often, non-financial or intangible considerations or intangible factors may affect the pricing of a target firm. These intangible values may not be recorded in the financial statements of the target firm. Some of these values may be unknown or underappreciated by the market. Several of the

---

[12]Geraldine Fabrikant, "Paramount-Viacom Talks Heat Up," *New York Times,* September 11,1993, L39.

[13]Ibid.

[14]Geraldine Fabrikant, "Paramount-Viacom Talk Lifts Stocks," *New York Times,* September 10, 1993, D2.

[15]Johnnie L. Roberts, "Paramount Net Increased 22% in Fiscal 4th Period," *Wall Street Journal,* January 22, 1993, C2, col. 3.

problems that come up after acquisitions may have been caused by valuations of the target directed only on market and financial statement values. Among the assets of target firms which may not be accounted for are:

1. Organizational employees whose skill and motivation propel the firm towards success.
2. Well-developed and efficient distribution system.
3. Reputation with customers and competitors, as well as its reputation for product quality and service.
4. Market share domination.
5. Government permits and approvals; demonstrated capability to meet government, industry, and customer standards and specifications.
6. Well-funded pension and other employee benefit plans.
7. Assets which are not currently needed but which are very liquid and may be easily sold or used as loan collateral.
8. Other synergy opportunities available which may not be uncovered during valuation.
9. Intellectual properties such as trade secrets.
10. Undervalued land, plant, equipment, and leases.
11. Terminable expenses such as management "perquisites" and unpromising discretionary projects.
12. Access to raw materials, energy, and transportation facilities and services.
13. Current contracts with suppliers and customers.
14. Agreements with franchise or distributorships.

In addition to the assets not appearing in the financial statements, there may also be liabilities which may not appear on the financial statements. Many consist of an absence or weakness in the assets described above.[16]

---

[16]Charles A. Scharf, Edward E. Shea, George C. Beck, *Acquisitions, Mergers, Sales, Buyouts and Takeovers: A Handbook with Forms,*(Englewood Cliffs, N.J.: Prentice Hall, 1985), 70.

Of course, all the above may not apply with a particular company. For example, in the case of Paramount-Viacom deal, synergistic values, well-developed and efficient distribution system were certainly some of the non-financial considerations that became apparent in the action. We find this hint in the statement of rival bidder QVC attacking Viacom's plans for Paramount as "nebulous talk about synergies and unspecified cutbacks."[17]

There were other subtle non-financial considerations in the Paramount-Viacom deal that were more personal in nature. For example, Viacom Mr. Redstone's desire for empire-building, which offered power and status because of size.[18] Managers may reap intangible benefits such as power and social status when they run large firms.[19] Also Viacom had an entrepreneurial environment that motivated it to undertake the acquisition.[20]

Unquestionably, clashes of egos, especially between Paramount's Mr. Davis, and rival bidder QVC's Mr. Diller were prominent in the action. As noted by one reporter, "it has [the takeover of Paramount] pitted former Paramount studio chief, Barry Diller, now [at the time of the transaction] chairman of QVC, against his former boss, Paramount chairman, Martin Davis,"[21] who, as QVC's Diller had charged in court, "appeared to have negotiated a friendly deal with Viacom in order to keep his company out of Mr. Diller's [Davis' former subordinate] hands."[22]

---

[17]Johnnie L. Roberts, and Randall Smith, "QVC Rules Out Altering Its Bid For Paramount," *Wall Street Journal*, February 14, 1994.

[18]Elizabeth Comte, "Giving Viewers A Choice," *Forbes*, January 4, 1993, 142.

[19]P.S. Sudarsanam, *The Essence of Mergers and Acquisitions*,(Cornwall, U.K.: Prentice Hall, 1995), 16-17.

[20]Comte, "Giving Viewers A Choice," *Forbes*, January 4, 1993, 142.

[21]Randall Smith, "Viacom Appears To Have Won Paramount War," Wall Street Journal, February 15, 1994, A3.

[22]Ibid., A9.

Chapter V

Analysis Of The Price Offered By Viacom To Acquire Paramount

Basic Principles Of Pricing

Unquestionably, the pricing issue of a target firm is the most painstaking decision that managers of both acquiring and target firms confront in negotiating an acquisition. This decision is painstaking due to the fact that several factors must be taken into consideration. For example, the future income stream or profitability of the target firm, the anticipated synergies, complicated tax rules, alternative legal ways of consummating the transaction, and accounting considerations, to name only a few, become involved.

To better appreciate the pricing of the Paramount-Viacom deal, a grasp of the basic principles involved in pricing a target firm is necessary. There are two basic principles: the "Investment Principle," and the "Alternatives Principle."[1]

---

[1]Raymond C. Miles, *How To Price A Business,*(Englewood Cliffs, NJ: Institute for Business Planning, 1985), 11-15.

Investment Principle

The Investment Principle states that a firm acquiring another firm involves more than a mere "expenditure." The purchase is an investment on which the acquirer should anticipate and receive a return for his investment. In other words, the acquirer should be entitled to expect a return or profit on his investment directly related to the purchase price and the level of risk anticipated.[2]

Alternatives Principle

This principle states that "the seller [target firm] and potential buyer [acquirer] of a business each have alternatives to consummating a sell-buy transaction with each other." In other words, the target company has alternatives as to whether to sell itself to a particular acquirer, or to sell itself at all. In the same vein, the acquiring company has alternatives as to acquire a particular target firm, or to utilize its excess cash in acquisition at all.[3] As mentioned previously(see chapter IV), alternatives exist for the acquirer with regards to the use of its excess cash. This alternative principle is sometimes overlooked during the bargaining phase of the pricing of a target. Both acquirer and target have alternatives to going ahead with a contemplated purchase/sell transaction.

The important point here is that both the acquiring firm and the target firm must be cognizant of all alternatives during the negotiations, so as to arrive at a well-informed agreement on an actual valuation and pricing decision.

---

[2]Raymond C. Miles, *How To Price A Business*,(Englewood Cliffs, NJ: Institute for Business Planning, 1985), 11-15.

[3]Ibid.

These two principles lead us into yet another principle, the "Investment Value-Concept."

Investment Value Concept

The Investment Value Concept is an offshoot of the Investment Principle and the Alternatives Principle, and it relates the two concepts. It can be construed as "the amount of investment in the business [target firm] at which the business would yield a specified rate of return on investment."[4] It expresses an interrelationship that exists among the following three variables:

1. The amount of return(profit)that the target firm provides.
2. The rate of return on investment.
3. The investment value of the business or target.

Of course, knowing any two of the variables can result in the determination of the third variable algebraically.

Thus,

$$\text{Investment Value} = \frac{\text{Amount of Return(profit)from Target Firm}}{\text{Rate of Return on Investment}}$$

where, the rate of return is expressed as a decimal form. The Investment Value concept takes on utmost importance in arriving at pricing decisions because it considers the acquirer or target firm's investment alternatives, as they may differ with regards to rate of return.[5] For example, a target firm earning a profit, or return on investment of $500,000 annually, with the target or acquiring firm's investment alternatives being such as to require a rate of return of

---

[4]Raymond C. Miles, *How To Price A Business*,(Englewood Cliffs, NJ: Institute for BusinessPlanning, 1985), 11-15.

[5]Ibid.

0.35(35 percent)from the target, will result in an approximate investment value of:

$$\text{Investment Value} = \frac{\$500,000}{0.35}$$

$$= \$1,428,571$$

This means that $1,428,571 is the highest that the target or acquirer
can invest in the business and still attain at least a 35 percent yearly
return on investment at the $500,000 annual profit. The investment value
concept is not necessarily the same as the purchase price of the target, nor
does it necessarily correspond with the target's actual market value.[6] As
previously stated, the investment value concept relates the Investment
Principle to the Alternatives Principle from the standpoint of pricing
a business.

There are two other points about the Investment Value that require
emphasis. The first is that one should not make the assumption that
the buyer's(acquirer's)investment value of a given firm has any particular relationship to the owner's(target's)actual investment in the firm.
The buyer's investment value is a function of the amount of return
from the firm and the rate of return on investment that is appropriate
under the circumstances.

Secondly, no single figure exists for the buyer's investment value of a
corporation. The value is only related to a function of opinion as to
future earnings, and the rate of return on investment that is considered
right, in light of both the nature of the firm and the alternatives available to the potential purchaser.[7]

---

[6]Raymond C. Miles, *How To Price A Business*,(Englewood Cliffs, NJ: Institute for
Business Planning, 1985), 11-15.

[7]Ibid., 59.

Price Paid By Viacom To Acquire Paramount

On March 11, 1994, Viacom purchased a majority of the shares(50.1 percent)of Paramount's common stock outstanding, at a price of $107 per share in cash. On July 7, 1994 Paramount became a completely owned subsidiary of Viacom. The total purchase price of $9.9 billion broke down as follows: $3.7 billion borrowed from banks, $3.1 billion of cash, and $3.1 billion of securities. The securities were included to offer shareholders extra compensation of the market price if Viacom stock did not increase to a specific level within a given period of time. The $3.1 billion of cash was procured through Viacom's issuance of $1.8 billion of Preferred stock(of which $600 million and $1.2 billion were issued to Blockbuster and Nynex Corporation, respectively)and $1.25 billion of Viacom's Class B Common Stock issued to Blockbuster. The securities issued to Blockbuster were subsequently canceled upon consummation of the Blockbuster merger with Viacom.[8]

As previously noted, the most important part of the analysis of an acquisition is the determination of the value of the target firm. These may be broadly categorized into those based on(1)earnings and assets, and(2)cash flows. The earnings and assets-based techniques are less information-intensive than the cash flow technique. The techniques distill under two main methods which are the Price to Earnings(P/E)Ratio method and the Discounted Cash Flow(DCF)method.[9]

---

[8]Securities and Exchange Commission, *Annual Report of Viacom Inc.(10-K)for the Fiscal Year Ended December 31, 1996*, Washington, D.C.

[9]P.S. Sudarsanam, *The Essence of Mergers and Acquisitions*,(London: Prentice Hall, 1995), 139, 150.

P/E Ratio Method

According to subscribers of the P/E ratio method of appraising the value of a target firm, the selling price of the target should be calculated in accordance to the relationship that the selling price of common stocks of the target bears to the annual earnings(profits)of the target firm. For example, if stock prices are in the neighborhood of four times annual earnings on a per-share basis, then a price equal to four times the annual profit would be appropriate for the target firm. This technique of valuation has some validity which essentially is premised upon the investment value concept. In a broad and general sense, some of this validity is traceable to the fact that the fluctuation of P/E ratios is somewhat related to overall business conditions and to investment yields in general. However, serious shortcomings of the P/E ratio method can be seen from the point of view of the Alternatives Principle discussed earlier in this chapter. In order for the P/E ratio technique to be valid from the viewpoint of the Alternative Principle, it would be necessary that the potential acquirer's principal alternative to buying the business would be to invest in the stock of another publicly-owned firm. This is not true in the majority of cases. The potential buyer is generally looking to take an active part in the management of the target. In fact, the potential buyer is seeking complete control in the target, so buying a stock in another public firm is not frequently a real alternative for the acquirer. Purchase of stock without the objective of acquiring the publicly-owned firm generally involves a small fraction of the firm's total ownership shares, whereas the buying of a company involves at least a controlling portion or complete ownership. This difference, by itself, accounts for very significant differences in prices paid.[10]

---

[10]Raymond C. Miles, *How To Price A Business*,(Englewood Cliffs, NJ: Institute for Business Planning, 1985), 9.

Discounted Cash Flow(DCF)Method

The Discounted Cash Flow(DCF)method is a simple Capital budgeting model, which discounts the estimated cash flows of the target firm at an estimated discount rate based upon the going market rate, the risk level of the target firm, and the risk-free Treasury Bill rate. To analyze whether the Paramount-Viacom deal was viable, we must determine the following:

1. The estimated discount rate to be used in discounting the cash flows of Paramount.
2. The estimated cash flow projections for Paramount.
3. The Present Value of Paramount cash flows at the estimated discount rate.

The risk-free rate is, for practical purposes, the return on a short-dated, such as 90 days, government Treasury Bill(T-Bill). The sensitivity of stock return to market return, called the Beta factor, is an estimation by an econometric forecasting that utilizes historic share price data. For publicly traded firms, betas are readily available from investment advisory services such as the *Value Line Investment Survey*. The discounted cash flow technique is applied in the following steps to evaluate a target:

1. Estimation of the future cash flows of Paramount based on the assumptions for its post-acquisition management by Viacom over the forecast horizon.
2. Estimation of the terminal value of Paramount at forecast horizon.
3. Estimation of the cost of capital appropriate for Paramount, given its pro-forma post-acquisition risk and capital structure.
4. Discounting of the estimated cash flows to give a value of Paramount.
5. Adding other cash inflows from sources such as asset disposals or business divestments.

6. Subtracting debt and other expenses, such as tax on gains from disposals and divestments, and acquisition costs, to give a value for the equity of Paramount.

7. Comparing the estimated equity value for Paramount with its pre-acquisition stand-alone value to determine the added value from the acquisition.

8. Deciding on how much of this added value should be given away to Paramount's shareholders as control premium.[11]

As mentioned previously, due to the fact that the P/E ratio method for pricing a business for sale has some serious shortcomings of which numerous professional analysts are apparently not aware, or choose to ignore,[12] this paper is going to employ the Discounted Cash Flow Technique to determine the valuation of Paramount at the time of the acquisition in 1994.

Thus, Estimated Discount Rate=(Rm-Rf)B+Rf

where,

Rm=market yield(prime rate)=6 percent[13]

Rf=risk-free(Treasury Bill rate)=2.97 percent[14]

Beta Factor(B)=post-acquisition beta factor=1.10[15]

---

[11]P. S. Sudarsanam, *The Essence of Mergers and Acquisitions,*(London: Prentice Hall, 1995), 150, 153.

[12]Raynold C. Miles. *How to Price a Business,*(Englewood Cliffs, NJ: Institute for Business Planning, 1985), 9.

[13]*New York Times*, September 10, 1993, D14.

[14]*New York Times*, September 10, 1993, D14.

[15]*Value Line Investment Survey*, March 30, 1997, 1786.

Substituting into above formula,

1. Estimated Discount rate=(6-2.97)1.10+2.97
=3.333+2.97
=6.303 percent≈6 percent or .06

2.Projected Cash Flows(in million of dollars):

	Current Yr.	Year 1	Year 2	Year 3	Year 4	Year 5
NIAT	220,000,000[16]	231,660,000	243,937,980	256,866,693	270,480,628	284,816,101
Retention (40%)	132,000,000	12,277,980	12,928,713	13,613,935	14,335,473	15,092,253
Cash Avail.	88,000,000	219,382,020	231,009,267	243,252,758	256,145,155	269,720,848

3. Terminal Value:

The terminal value is based upon the constant growth of the final year's estimated cash flows for Paramount.

Final Year's cash flows=269,720,848

where,   K=.06, n=5

Therefore,

$$\text{Terminal value}=\frac{\text{Year 5 cash flow x PVIF}_n,K}{K}$$

---

[16]*Forbes*, January 3, 1994, p. 143(at 5.3 percent growth rate).

$$\underline{\frac{269,720,848 \times .7473}{.06}}$$
$$= 3,359 \text{ million}$$

Thus, the **net cash flows** are as follows(in millions of dollars):

	Cash Avail. To Viacom	Terminal Value	Total Cash Flow		Discount Factor	Present Value
Year 1	219,382,020		219,382,020	x	.9434	206,964,998
Year 2	231,009,267		231,009,267	x	.8900	205,598,248
Year 3	243,252,758		243,252,758	x	.8396	204,235,016
Year 4	256,145,155		256,145,155	x	.7921	202,892,577
Year 5	269,720,848	+3,359	3,629,094,010	x	.7473	2,712,021,954

Present Value=$3,531,712,793

Unquestionably, with Paramount's 1994 estimated market value being **$3,531,712,793** and the actual price paid by Viacom being **$9.9 billion**, a vast difference existed in the valuation of Paramount. This leads us to examine yet another principle of valuation, the substitution principle, to attempt to find out what other factors may have influenced the high purchase price for Paramount by Viacom. Of course, it is quite evident by now that synergistic benefits and the bidding war contributed significantly to hiking Paramount's market value. But to what extent, and how synergistic appraisals are approximated, is the subject of this last section of this chapter.

Substitution Principle

The Substitution Principle states that "the value of a thing tends to be determined by the cost of acquiring an equally desirable substitute."[17] The principle is related to the "market data approach" to estimating value, and may also be called "market comparison approach." This relationship of the substitution principle and the market data approach stems from the fact that the market data approach derives its theoretical basis in the substitution principle.[18]

In determining the valuation of a business by the market comparison technique, the valuer tries to identify other businesses that fall within the desired line of business that have actually been sold. The valuer then utilizes information about the selling price of the business that has been sold as a basis of valuation for the business being appraised.[19] The closer the time frame that the comparable businesses fall within, the less room there is for inaccuracies in the valuation. In other words, due to the inherent uncertainty about the appropriate percentage adjustment to apply, to reflect differences in time of sale, the adjustment process becomes less accurate as the time difference widens. For this reason, the time differences between the date of each comparable sale and the effective date of the appraisal must be as close as possible to offset such factors as inflation and actual changes in price levels in the market for the particular kind of business being appraised. Preferably, the required adjustment for time of sale should perhaps fall in the range of 10-20 percent.[20]

It may be quite likely that the huge purchase price Viacom paid for the acquisition of Paramount, compared with its estimated market

---

[17]Raymond C. Miles, *Basic Business Appraisal,*(New York: John Wiley & Sons, 1984), 161.

[18]Ibid.

[19]Ibid., 162.

[20]Ibid., 181, 182.

value, may have been due to the appraisal of intangibles. Even before QVC entered the bidding war that ultimately raised the price of Paramount to $9.9 billion, Paramount's friendly deal with Viacom was $8.2 billion, a figure which was still quite high in comparison to the estimated market value of Paramount. such an analysis falls outside the scope of this book, since our objective is to attempt to determine the economic prudence of the action as reflected in Viacom today.

Placing a value on a business's intangibles can represent one of the most difficult, and in a sense least rewarding, applications of the market data approach. This is so due to:

1. The difficulties involved in identifying sales of businesses reasonably alike to the business being valued.
2. Problems in getting enough information pertaining to some or all of the comparable sales that are identified.
3. Constraints inherent in the adjustment process as a tool for compensating or rectifying the differences between the business being appraised and the comparable business, including circumstances and terms of sale in addition to differences between the business themselves.[22]

For example, there may be such differences as capital structure, historical growth rate, size of business, profitability, competitive position, to name only few of these countless variations.

These reasons, perhaps, led to such a wide discrepancy between our estimated market value of Paramount and the price that Viacom actually paid. But to really get to the complete factors, especially the intangibles, that led to the high appraisal of Paramount, taking into account the so-called "trade secrets," may prove futile. Most importantly, such an analysis falls outside the scope of this research paper, since our objective is to attempt to determine the economic prudence of the action as reflected in Viacom today.

---

[22]Raymond C. Miles, *Basic Business Appraisal*,(New York: John Wiley, 1984), 182.

Chapter VI

Viacom Incorporation's Financial Condition Before, During, And After

To analyze Viacom's financial position prior to, during, and after the transaction, it is necessary that we examine two factors that influence the price that the acquirer pays for a target firm. Unquestionably, the higher the amount that drains out of the acquirer's coffers, the higher it becomes weakened financially, and vice versa. These two factors are,(1)the role of investment bankers in acquisitions, and(2)the role of rival bidders in acquisitions.

Role Of Investment Bankers

In actual acquisition situations, firms frequently hire investment banking firms to assist in developing not only the valuation estimates of target firms, but also the acquirer's financial position. Major investment banking firms have merger and acquisition groups that operate within their corporate finance departments. Investment bankers strive to identify companies with excess cash that might want to acquire other firms. They also offer packages of financing to corporate acquirers, with the package including both the design of securities used.[1] For example, General Electric hired Morgan Stanley toestimate a fair price for Utah International; in the same vein, Royal Dutch also hired Morgan Stanley to assist in determining the price it paid for Shell Oil. Even if the takeover is not a friendly one, investment bankers may still be hired to assist in determining a price. If a surprise tender offer is to be made, the acquirer will want to find out the lowest price at which it might be able to acquire the stock of the target, whereas the target company may also want to find out its fair market price to prove that the acquirer's price being offered for it is too low.

Of course, such determinations by investment bankers are shrouded in secrecy. For if it becomes public knowledge that, say, firm X was contemplating offering $40 per share for firm Y, which was currently selling at $30 per share, people could make huge profits. One of the biggest of such huge amassing of profits, called insider trading, which became a scandal on Wall Street in the 1980s, was the disclosure that a well-known investor, Ivan Boesky, was purchasing from a senior member, Dennis Levine, of the investment banking firm Drexel Burnham Lambert, information about prospective acquisitions of firms his company Drexel was analyzing for others. Boesky's purchases hiked the prices of the stocks and thus forced Drexel's acquirer client to pay more than it would have otherwise had to pay.[2] The point here is, the financial condition of an acquirer in the acquisition process can be significantly affected by the work of investment bankers. For example, as briefly mentioned a while ago, when an acquirer overpays during an acquisition, it becomes deprived

---

[1]Fred J. Weston, Eugene F. Brigham, *Essentials of Managerial Finance*, 10th Ed.,(New York: Dryden Press, 1993), 844-845.
[2]Ibid.

of funds which otherwise could have gone into reducing other costs such as huge fees that are frequently incurred in takeover attempts. Even if the acquisition is fended off, costs are incurred. When, at one point before its takeover by Viacom, Paramount Communications attempted to acquire Time, it incurred about $50 million in its failed attempt, and Time's costs to ward off Paramount and to acquire Warner were over $100 million.[3]

The knowledge of investment bankers is quite impressive in the corporate takeover arena, and with knowledge comes power and influence to affect finances of an acquirer adversely or constructively. Among them are:

1. Knowledge of business available for sale.
2. Knowledge of acquirers looking to undertake acquisitions.
3. Knowledge of terms of recently consummated transactions.
4. Knowledge of the availability and terms of acquisition.
5. The ability to raise financing by underwriting public offerings or acting as agents for private placements.
6. The ability to furnish or arrange bridge loans for some acquisitions.
7. Knowledge of financial analysis of acquisition candidates
8. Knowledge of business analysis of acquisition candidates.
9. Advising in structuring acquisitions including introductions. to legal, accounting, and tax experts.
10. Knowledge of developing government policies.
11. Conducting divestiture "auctions."
12. Fairness options.
13. Advising on negotiating strategies and conducting negotiations, when requested.[4]

---

[3]Ibid.

[4]Charles A. Scharf, Edward E. Shea, and George C. Beck., *Acquisitions, Mergers, Sales, Buyouts and Takeovers*, 4th ed.,(Englewood Cliffs: NJ, 1991), 49-50.

Each step along these functions, improperly executed, could be detrimental to the finances of an acquirer. For example, using knowledge to advise on a wrong business to purchase could lead to the acquirer making a poor investment. In the same way, using knowledge to ill-advise(contrary to ethics)an acquirer of terms of recent transactions could also lead to dire financial consequences for the acquirer.

With the above functions of investment bankers noted, it can readily be seen that they can significantly affect for good or for ill the financial position of not only the acquiring firm, but also the target firm as well.

Role of Rival Bidders

Next to investment bankers in influence that could adversely affect the financial condition of an acquirer in the corporate takeover process, as we noted earlier, is rival bidders. In the Paramount-Viacom transaction, the influence that rival bidder, QVC, exerted on the purchase price of Paramount is quite evident. It hiked the price that Viacom originally intended to pay from $8.2 billion to $9.9 billion, generating a premium of $1.7 billion. This was a whopping amount that could have otherwise gone into reducing some of the acquisition fees. Corporate takeovers, in this sense, are in every aspect similar to an auction. The absence of a rival bidder means the purchase price of a firm will remain the same, or could even drop from what a target company initially announces, such as in a friendly deal. Conversely, the presence of a rival bidder is certain to increase the purchase price. For example, it is quite likely that if QVC had not emerged in the transaction, Viacom could have argued that the price that Paramount was asking probably did not reflect the lower market value of Paramount, and may have succeeded in getting Paramount to reduce it. In friendly deals, such as the Paramount-Viacom deal, both negotiating parties may allow for some increment of the price of the target above their own agreed "true" market value. This increment may be intentionally designed to reduce the number of rival bidders, or to discourage other potential entrants to the transaction who may find the high price unaffordable.

Viacom's Financial Condition

The schedule appearing below depicts Viacom's financial condition as compared with its sub-industry of broadcasting and cable median, two years prior to its takeover of Paramount.

Table 6.1: Viacom's Financial Condition against Industry Median.

Profitability				Growth				Sales	Net Income	Profit Margin
Return on Equity				Sales		Earnings/Share				
5-Yr Avg %	Latest 12 mos %	Return on capital latest 12 mos %	Debt/ capital %	5-yr avg %	Latest 12 mos %	5-yr avg %	Latest 12 mos %	Latest 12 mos $ mil	Latest 12 mos $ mil	Latest 12 mos %
January 6, 1992										
def+	def	2.7	76.4	25.6	8	NA	D-D	1679	-105	def
January 4, 1993										
def*	3.4	7.4	78.2	14.1	8.2	NM	D-P	1816	26	1.4
January 3, 1994										
def	20.5	9	73.6	12.4	9.3	NM	500.0+	1986	155	7.8

Industry Median (Broadcasting and Cable)

January 6, 1992										
def	def	2.8	84.7	29.1	8	NM	D-D	1442	-105	-5.3
January 4, 1993										
def	0.9	8.1	78.7	15.4	7	NM	5.3	1229	39	3.5
January 3, 1994										
def	13	9.2	69.2	12.1	11.2	NM	18.8	1594	76	6.1

D-D: Deficit to deficit   **D-P:** Defit to profit   **def:** Deficit
NA: Not applicable   **NM:** Not meaningful   **+:** Four-year average
***:** Three-year average

(Sources: Forbes 1/6/92, p. 142. 1/4/93, p. 143, 1/3/94, p. 143)
Value Line database service via Lotus Co. Investment.

Under profitability in the schedule, return on equity, which measures the rate of return on common stockholders' investment, Viacom registered deficits of 3.4 percent and 20.5 percent against industry median deficits of 0.9 percent and 13.0 percent for 1993, and 1994 respectively. This trend, especially the dramatic improvement in 1994 of 7.5 percent above the industry median, showed an efficient financial management. Viacom saw earnings growth per share of 500.0+ percent against a very scanty industry average of 18.8 percent in 1994. The company's profit margin on sales, which measures income per dollar of sales, showed a marked improvement of 7.8 percent against industry median of 6.1 percent in 1994. However, the rosy financial picture was to change during and after the acquisition of Paramount. This condition was largely a result of the intense bidding war that rival bidder, QVC, presented to Viacom.

During the bidding contest for Paramount, Viacom's investment bankers at Smith Barney Shearson said, "Viacom expected annual cost savings of $200 million at the minimum from, among other things, elimination of duplicate television production, distribution and sales, as well as savings on overhead and administration costs."[5] The post-acquisition period saw Viacom becoming "heavily laden with debt,"[6]

---

[5]Laura Landro, "Viacom Names Team to Consolidate Assets of Paramount and Blockbuster," *Wall Street Journal*, March 16, 1994, B4.

[6]Ibid.

and according to Wall Street analysts, expected "Viacom management to take $250 million in pretax restructuring charges that include staff cutbacks in corporate and operations areas."

Chapter VII

Post-Acquisition Analysis Of Viacom And The Industry

Before we go on to the analysis of Viacom after its 1994 acquisition of Paramount, it might be useful to learn some basic concepts about immediate post-acquisition process and the integration of two combined companies.

Integrating the Acquired Firm

The time period immediately following the closing of an acquisition is very critical, when steps must be taken to integrate the acquired firm by the acquirer. Within a few months, skillful acquirers will put in place plans aimed at realizing the synergies that were the goals of the takeover . Conversely, some acquirers will sow the seeds that can result in the disintegration of the acquired firm. This is also the period when a variety of accounting, legal, tax, employee benefits, and other integral steps must be initiated because they may later become difficult, if not impossible to implement, to ensure the success of the combined companies.[1]

---

[1]Charles A. Scharf, Edward E. Shea, and George C.Beck, *Acquisitions, Mergers, Sales, Buyouts and Takeovers*, 4th ed.,(Englewood Cliffs, NJ: Prentice Hall, 1991),505.

Unquestionably, one of the principal objectives of corporate combinations centers on the primacy of cost-reduction by elimination of duplicate facilities and work forces. Of course, this may be injurious to competition and may attract the scrutiny of antitrust regulators. History has shown that corporate combinations were seldom successful unless programs apart from cost reductions alone were introduced. Cost reductions are not a main objective for most acquisitions, but opportunities exist after most acquisitions. Some are virtually automatic. For example, after a publicly owned corporation is taken over, the need for its public and shareholder relations department ceases to exist, along with part of the work done by its accounting, legal, and other departments because this functions fall on the appropriate departments of the acquirer. It is necessary that every essential cost cutting program be part of a credible turnaround and future growth program, or it is bound to be a failure. For example, if employees know that a firm's products or processes have fallen into technological obsolescence, they will want to see that cost cutting will be applied to a realistic modernization program. Otherwise, they will believe that the cost cuttings will only delay the inevitable disintegration of the acquired company, and they may offer resistance to extra work and other sacrifices. A cost cutting program should also be intelligent and fair in its administration. Getting rid of productive departments and people in the seller organization in favor of weaker departments and people in the buyer organization will come across to employees as organizational "politics," with the consequence of weak employee morale.[2]

Some experts on post-acquisition integration recommend that in order to skillfully, integrate acquisitions the following considerations must be taken into account:

---

[2]Charles A. Scharf, Edward E. Shea, and George C.Beck, *Acquisitions, Mergers, Sales, Buyouts and Takeovers*, 4th ed.,(Englewood Cliffs, NJ: Prentice Hall, 1991),505.

1. Planners should be aware that every acquisition involves integration, even when the acquirer promises extensive autonomy to management of the acquired firm. For example, financial reporting, budgets, cash management, taxes, insurance, general personnel policies, employee benefits and other activities commonly come under one umbrella even when the acquired firm is successful and will have operational freedom.
2. The top management of the seller firm should ascertain whether they can work within the acquired's management structure which will inevitably dictate some degree of review and approval of their decisions
3. The acquirer's methods should not be imposed on the acquired firm's operations until the working professionals in both combining companies have exchanged visits to each of their workplaces and have come to agreement as to the advantages and disadvantages of the existing methods employed for each company.
4. Acquired firm's management should initiate steps directed at integration by early involvement of its operational personnel, preferably during the "due diligence" review or audit.
5. The acquirer should refrain from forcing integration of businesses that initially seem to be similar, but experience shows are not.[3]

Among the most essential post acquisition strategies are:

1. Open sharing by senior management in hard work, risk, and austerity budgetary measures.
2. Implementation of personnel cutting over a short time frame, followed by significant bonus and incentive programs

---

[3]Ibid., 506.

for remaining employees asked to and given freedom to assume additional responsibilities.

3. Utilization of funds created for saving, even when still scarce, to purchase long-needed equipment to improve product or service quality and efficiency.

4. Carefully listening and planning to match cost reductions burdens on productivity.

5. Continually stressing the fact to employees that their contributions to the combined business will be recognized and rewarded. Real awards for achievements by both operating and administrative workers must be given by top management.

6. Reduction of bureaucracy by accountability systems including replacement of managers who prove incapable of developing and successfully carrying out improvements, or who strangulate employee innovation and growth.[4]

With the foregoing considerations in mind, we shall see that Viacom's success or failure would stem from its cognizance of these considerations.

Post-Acquisition Analysis of Viacom

Immediately following the acquisition, Viacom began naming its teams to consolidate the assets of not only Paramount but Blockbuster as well. Viacom said the transition team would include two of its executives and one from Paramount, all of whom would report to Viacom's president and chief execute officer, Mr. Frank Biondi. Viacom General counsel, Mr. Philippe P. Dauman, would become vice-president and chief administrative officer, while Mr. Thomas E. Dooley, who was the

---

[4]Charles A. Scharf, Edward E. Shea, and George C.Beck, *Acquisitions, Mergers, Sales, Buyouts and Takeovers*, 4th ed.,(Englewood Cliffs, NJ: Prentice Hall, 1991),505.

head of Viacom's corporate development, would be executive vice-president of finance, corporate development and communications. Mr. Martin Davis, Paramount's chairman, and Mr. Stanley Jaffe, Paramount's president, would leave their executive posts but remain to work informally on the management transition. Paramount's formal representative on the transition team was Mr. Ronald L. Nelson who was executive vice-president and chief financial officer. Wall Street analysts expected Viacom, which was heavily laden with debt, to sharply cut staffing levels in such areas as Television distribution, where Viacom, Paramount, and Blockbuster combined had four different overlapping units.[5]

During the week of January 15, 1996, two years after the acquisition, Viacom's chairman Mr. Sumner Redstone, fired Mr. Frank Biondi, his long-running chief executive officer, and grabbed the post for himself, jolting Hollywood and capping what apparently was a quietly building struggle over management style and company bottom-line results. That raised the question of whether Viacom could thrive with Mr. Redstone in the sole starring role. Mr. Redstone cited Paramount's recent poor performance as one of the main reasons for Mr. Biondi's dismissal.[6] Viacom's latest proxy statement reported that Biondi would receive payments totaling more than $15 million to terminate his contract.[7]

In the first quarter of 1996 Viacom's earnings declined 61 percent to $27.8 million, from $71.2 million a year earlier. The problem was its entertainment division which included Paramount filmed entertainment, where Mr. Biondi had been the head.[8] Following Viacom's long-delayed

---

[5]Laura Landro, "Viacom Names Team to Consolidate Assests of Paramount and Blockbuster," *Wall Street Journal*, March 16, 1994, B4.

[6]John Lippman, "Paramount Feeling the Heat in Wake of Biondi Firing," *Wall Street Journal*, January 22, 1996, B4, Col. 3.

[7]Jeffrey A. Trachtenberg, "Biondi to Receive $15 million to end Pact With Viacom," *Wall Street Journal*, April 15, 1996, B4, Col. 6.

[8]Eben Shapiro, "Viacom's Earnings Skid 61%, Hurt By 2 Major Units," *Wall Street Journal*, May 6, 1996, B6, Col. 6.

plan to shed its cable systems in a transaction valued at $2.3 billion, as part of a plan to reduce its heavy debt of $11 billion, it finally announced its debt would be cut by $1.7 billion.[9]

The second quarter of 1996 saw Viacom's profit dropping by 22 percent to $41.1 million from a year earlier, amid lackluster results from most of its core business, including its entertainment operations, where cash flow weakened despite the strong box-office performance of Paramount's "Mission: Impossible." Viacom's cash flow-or its earnings before interest, taxes, depreciation, and amortization, a closely watched indicator of an entertainment firm's performance-fell 15 percent to $468.2 million.[10]

A press report commented in the latter part of 1996 that Viacom had pretty cheap stock, but its financial performance had not fulfilled the promise and hype of the original merger documents, which included projected financial statements outlining how the firm would have done if the acquisition transaction had taken place a year earlier, and suggesting the path of its future growth.[11]

In a speech made on December 13, 1996 at a Paine Webber Inc. media conference, Viacom Chairman Mr. Redstone proclaimed plans were afoot to cut down its debt burden by 20 percent or more to between $6 billion and $8 billion in the next two to three years from about $10 billion, a debt taken on as a result of the company's 1994 buying of Paramount and Blockbuster, as part of efforts to rejuvenate its falling stock price.[12]

---

[9]Staff Reporter, "Viacom Starts Offer To Exchange Shares Related to Cable Sale," *Wall Street Journal*, June 25, 1996, C15, Col. 3.

[10]Eben Shapiro, "Viacom 2nd Period Profit Skidded 22% On Lackluster Results At Most Core Lines," *Wall Street Journal*, August 1, 1996, B14, Col. 1.

[11]Linda Sandler, "Viacom's Promises For Rosy Financial Benefits From Mergers Failed to Include Few Thorns," *Wall Street Journal*, August 5, 1996, C2, Col. 3.

[12]Eben Shapiro, "Viacom to Reduce Debt Load In Move To Boost Its Stock," *Wall Street Journal*, December 16, 1996, B10, Col. 5.

On May 7, 1997, Viacom reported first quarter revenues of $2.9 billion, earnings before interest, taxes, depreciation, and amortization (EBITDA)of $392 million and operating income of $174 million. This compared to its 1996 period revenues of $2.6 billion, EBITDA of $448 million, and operating income of $256 million. The company reported growth in revenue in every sector, led by double-digit gains at MTV Networks, Blockbuster Video and Paramount's motion picture and television operations. For the first quarter of 1997, Viacom also reported a net loss from continuing operations of $24 million, or a loss of $.11 per stock share, against net earnings from continuing operations of $19 million, or $.01 per stock share in the same period in 1996. Its entertainment revenues increased 14 percent to $1.0 billion, with Paramount's television programming revenues increment due principally to its addition of new first run shows such as "Viper" and "Real TV," coupled with higher license fees and increased volume of network production.[13]

Viacom's management began to exhibit keen and prudent management practices. For example, the 1997 first quarter net loss from continuing operations of $24 million, or a loss of $.11 per stock share, may have prompted the management into considering a divestiture program when it announced it was putting up its Simon & Schuster publishing business, inherited from Paramount, for sale in an effort to "reduce its debt and focus on its core entertainment businesses, which include Paramount Communications, MTV and Nickelodeon."[14] This announcement resulted in the appreciation of Viacom's stock because investors perceived the company was making considerable efforts to reduce its heavy debt.

---

[13]George S. Smith, Jr., Vaughan A. Clark, and Christina Hornbeck, "Viacom Reports First Quarter 1997 Revenues of $2.9 billion, EBITDA of $392 million and Operating Income of $174 million," *News From Viacom*, May 7, 1997, 1.

[14]Geraldine Fabrikant, "Viacom May Form Joint Venture For Simon & Schuster Trade Unit," *New York Times*, January 22, 1998, D9.

Post-acquisition Analysis of the Entertainment Industry

After spending billions of dollars over the first two years after the Paramount-Viacom deal in 1994 on megamergers and consolidation, the entertainment firms were performing like some of Hollywood's bad movies. Giant companies like Walt Disney, Time Warner, and Viacom were struggling with various combinations of heavy debt burden, management problems, and questions pertaining to the best way to integrate their sprawling empires. A Salomon Brothers index of six entertainment stocks was up just 12 percent for the period from mid-1995 to mid-1996, compared with a 26 percent increase in the Standard & Poor's(S&P)400 Index. Used to the free-spending culture of Hollywood and pursuing growth through acquisitions, executives at many entertainment companies lacked experience managing in a more competitive, slower-growth environment. They also remained among the highest-paid executives in corporate America.[15]

The majority of the entertainment mergers and acquisitions were undertaken on the theory that growth is guaranteed if companies can control both distribution and programming(for example, ownership of a movie studio and a television network or cable system). But owning distribution does not seem critical now, due to the fact that phone companies and direct satellite services are now competing with cable operators, anxious to carry anyone's content. To make a bad situation worse, the Internet is siphoning off viewer time for television, depressing advertising sales for the broadcast networks. But the primacy of the U.S. culture globally remains a key strength of the industry. The entertainment industry is still one area where the U.S.

---

[15]Laura Landro, and Eben Shapiro, "Entertainment-Industry Outlook Is a Tearjerker," *Wall Street Journal*, July 9, 1996, B1, Col. 3.

continues to enjoy substantial competitive advantage. For example, within the U.S., foreign-made entertainment seldom achieves mass appeal for a sustained period, with the exception of British rock music. The global demand for U.S. entertainment is so high that countries ranging from Canada to France to Iran have made efforts to restrict the import of it, for various reasons.[16]

According to Entertainment Data, Inc., box office tallies through mid-December 1997 showed a more than 5 percent increase over the 1996 figure. But as mentioned earlier, the top executives and the stars coupled with high initial fixed cost of production managed to siphon off the money as quickly as the paying customers brought it in. Movie stocks underperformed the market by 14 percent in 1997, according to Salomon Smith Barney analyst Jill Krutick.[17] The entertainment industry has always favored large players, and the advancement of technology is always creating opportunities for synergies that can best be exploited by large firms.[18] But the entertainment industry is-as ever-always in a flux.[19] Perhaps, the experience of the four major companies-Walt Disney, Time Warner, Seagram, and Viacom-could better illustrate the uncertainties that surround the industry with regards to their quest for largeness and its attendant operational and financial efficiencies:

1. In 1995, Walt Disney announced acquisition of Capital Cities/ABC for $19 billion. The dream was to create unrivaled opportunities to promote Disney's movies, stores and theme

---

[16]Ben Sharav, "Entertainment Industry," *Value Line Investment Survey*, November 28,1997, 1789.

[17]Robert La Franco, "Entertainment and Information," *Forbes*, January 12, 1998, 148.

[18]Ben Sharav, "Entertainment Industry," *Value Line Investment Survey*, November 28, 1997, 1787.

[19]Robert La Franco, *Forbes*, 149.

parks on ABC and assure distribution for Disney's television shows. The reality was ABC's rating slid, consuming top management's time and leading to turmoil at the network. Studio performance became rocky, forcing cuts in production.

2. In 1995, Time Warner agreed to purchase Turner Broadcasting System for $7.5 billion in stock. The dream was that Time Warner's tremendous investment in cable systems would marry perfectly with Turner's cable programming prowess. The reality was that the deal became stalled in regulatory purgatory, with the Federal Trade Commission(FTC)concerned about concentration of programming and distribution power.

3. In 1995, Seagram announced acquisition of 80 percent of MCA for $5.7 billion. The dream was that energetic new management from Seagram would bring back luster to a faded entertainment conglomerate, that simply running MCA better would lead to higher profits. The reality was that MCA continued to lack powerful distribution outlets such as network or large cable systems. Additionally, fixing businesses turned out to consume more time and money than Wall Street expected.

4. In 1994, Viacom acquired Paramount and Blockbuster for a combined purchase price of $17.4 billion. The dream was that worldwide expansion of MTV and Paramount, fueled by massive cash flow of video rental business, and synergy between MTVnetworks, Paramount studios and Simon and Schuster book publisher would make the whole greater than the parts, or the so-called "2 plus 2 equals 5 effect." The reality was that concerns about Blockbuster's growth prospects haunted Viacom's stock. Wall Street was rattled by firing of Chief Executive Officer Frank Biondi in January of 1996, and

the lack of a designated successor to the aging chairman Mr. Sumner Redstone.[20]

As *Wall Street Journal* staff writers put it concisely, "every year about this time [July], media and entertainment executives flock to Sun Valley, Idaho, for the Allen and Co. investors conference to fish, hike and make deals. Walt Disney Co.'s $19 billion purchase of Capital Cities/ABC Inc. was hatched behind the scenes at the conference last year [1995]. But this year [1996], deals may be the last thing on anyone's mind. The talk of Sun Valley is likely to be how entertainment stocks have lost their sizzle.[21]

Perhaps, it is about time that entertainment companies dwelled awhile in their current houses of "2 plus 2 equals 5 effect," and consolidated what is in hand so far, rather than looking for new ones.

[20]Laura Landro, and Eben Shapiro, "Entertainment-Industry Outlook Is a Tearjerker," *Wall Street Journal*, July 9, 1996, B1, Col. 2 & 3.

[21]Ibid.

Chapter VIII

The Future Of The Entertainment And Information Industry

The future of the entertainment and information industry, akin to the saying that the message cannot be separated from the messenger, is really the future of the telecommunications industry. In order to have a clear vision of what the future holds for the telecommunications industry, it may be helpful that we explore the factors that areworking to condition the telecommunications industry.

Several factors have combined to result in the industry gravitating towards a convergence. The impact of this convergence is altering even the very name and meaning of entertainment and information to a degree. As we just shortly noted, the entertainment and information industry's name is increasingly becoming synonymous with telecommunication, the result of bold steps taken in optical fiber, digital television, video switching, and related technologies.

These factors shaping the telecommunications industry may be grouped under three main headings:(1)Effects of Competition, (2)Technological Advancements, and(3)Effects of the Demanding Public. We discuss each in turn.

Effects of Competition

The entertainment and information industry, and for that matter the telecommunications industry, as already mentioned in Chapter II, is immunized from general economic volatilities. This ability to withstand the general economic ups and downs makes it a very stable and lucrative industry to be in. This creates a tendency for the industry to attract swarms of start-up business capital seeking avenues of investment returns. In the same vein, entrenched firms in the industry are also investing huge capital outlays in Research and Development(R&D)towards innovation, in order to maintain their competitive advantages and industry leadership. The scrambling of firms for a piece of the action, and the working of a free and entrepreneurial marketplace where firms and combinations of firms are rushing to be first, have rendered the industry very dynamic and ultra-competitive.

Rapid and continuous changes are occurring in the industry by the hour, so to say. One only has to take a look at the accelerated pace at which the mediums of delivery of entertainment products reach maturity levels, and this fact becomes self evident. No sooner has a new medium or means of delivery of entertainment product been introduced in the market place, than it quickly falls into obsolescence. For example, the movie theater, revenues, were quickly siphoned off with the advent of the regular television shows, which in turn suffered the same fate with the introduction of cable television shows. Now, cable television shows. Now, cable television revenue is witnessing a siphoning off with the introduction of the satellite dish.

Firms are increasingly becoming aware that in order to keep pace with this spate of innovative demands necessary for their survival, they have to devise some kind of a link or union of the mediums of delivery of entertainment products, hence this convergence in the telecommunications industry. These fierce innovative demands are even more compounded by the movement towards globalization, and the universal nature and appeal of the U.S. culture is not being of much help either.

Globalization of business, or international business now comprises a large and growing portion of the world's total business. Today, you would be hard-pressed to find a company-large or small-that is not affected by global events and competition because most companies sell output to and/or secure supplies from foreign countries and/or compete against products and services that come from abroad. Companies are engaging in international business for three primary reasons:(a)Expansion of Sales,(b)Resource Acquisitions, and(c)Diversification of Sources of Sales. We explore these reasons further:[1]

(a)Expansion of Sales

Firms' sales of their products are dependent on two factors. The first factor is the consumers' interest in the firms' products and services and their ability to purchase them.

The global population and their purchasing power far outnumbers that of a single country, so firms may expand their sales by defining certain markets in international terms.

Ordinarily, more sales translate into higher profits. For example, Walt Disney promotes its U.S. theme parks in Latin America in order to increase the number of park visitors, and Disney's total revenues increase with additional admission or hotel space that is sold to Latin American tourists. Disney films such as "Aladdin" and "Beauty and the Beast" cost millions of dollars to produce; but as more and more people see the films, the average production cost per viewer declines.[2] The

---

[1]John D. Daniels, and Lee H. Radebaugh. *International Business: Environments and Operations.* 7th Ed., Addison-Wesley Publishing Company, 1995, New York, 9.
[2]Ibid.

opportunity to expand sales is thus a major motivation for a firm's expansion into the international arena.

Many of the world's largest firms obtain over half of their sales from outside their home country. With the U.S. culture having such a world-wide appeal, it is only natural that the future for the industry would continue to be one of global expansion.

(b)Resource Acquisitions

Producers and Distributors are constantly seeking out products and services.Producers also look for cheaper manufacturing bases. Sometimes they do this to cutdown on their production costs. For example, Disney depends on cheap manufacturing bases in China and Taiwan to supply clothing to its souvenir outlets.[3] The potentialre-wards of this logical move obvious: Either the profit margin may be increased or the cost savings may be passed on to consumers, who will in turn buy more products, thus resulting in increased profits through greater sales volume.

(c)Diversification of Sources of Sales

To help avoid wild swings in sales and profits, and to stabilize earnings, firms are seeking out foreign markets and sources of supplies. Several firms take advantage of the fact that the business cycles, that is, recessions and expansions differ among countries. For example, sales may decrease in a country that is experiencing economic recession and increase in one that is undergoing economic expansion.

Competition is, therefore, steering the entertainment and information industry, andfor that matter, the telecommunications industry into creativity at a breakneck pace. With the U.S. already a technological

---

[3]Michael Duckworth, "Disney Plans to Re-enter China Market As Beijing Promises Copyright Reforms," *Wall Street Journal*, March 24, 1992, C19.

genius and a pace-setter for the rest of the world, as measured by its cultural representation, it appears that the sky is the limit as to where the industry can reach. The drive for innovations in the industry is not a matter of just innovations for innovations sake. It is a matter of survival in this so-called information age, where technology spreads so quickly among nations. This fact becomes obvious especially in military armaments; as soon as any country gains monopoly over a military weaponry technology, it becomes quickly copied by another country, as evidenced in the current proliferation of nuclear weapons. Similar copying occurs in the entertainment and information industry as well. Sometimes some of these countries, in their zeal to become more competitive, engage in forms of competition not played by the rules, and which are quite difficult to enforce due to the cross-border dimensions involved. They may engage in outright piracy of the so-called intellectual property. China, for example, although ithas more recently made deep reforms in its copyright laws, readily comes to mind when the subject of copyright piracy is mentioned. But China may not be the only culprit in this breach of international copyright laws. Perhaps, most of these breaches are committed by the so-called lesser developed nations. China may have been singled out prominently because of its huge population size-over 1.2 billion. This means that for every intellectual property such as a song or screenplay that is pirated by China, the country has a large enough local market for it to seriously undermine the revenues of the original copyright owner, and thus presents a formidable competitive threat to these owners. Added to this,China has emerged as a technologically advanced country enough to offer a high quality product delivery system for its market, making piracy even more detrimental to the original copyright owners.

It appears that the problem of intellectual property piracy is far from being stemmed. For no matter how committed a country's copyright enforcement authorities may be, how can they really distinguish the original product from the duplicate? For example, how can a song accurately copied on a disk, or a formatted film duplicated on a video cassette by the original copyright owner, be distinguished form the original if the pirates copy these with the aid of technology? It is therefore logical that the only way the copyright owners could stay ahead of the competition is to continually come out with innovations after a brief monopoly reign. We now turn our attention to how technology is affecting this convergence of the industry.

Technological Advancement

The effects of competition alone in shaping the convergence in the entertainment and information industry will be grossly underestimated if the mention of technological advancement and its effect is left out of the picture. Technology is constantly forging a dramatic growth and evolution in the industry.

A pause to reflect on the nature of the entertainment and information industry and the product it produces, be it a screenplay or a song, quickly makes it self evident that without the technological advancements that have taken place, the entertainment and information industry is in several respects similar to the saying that the message cannot be divorced from the messenger. For example, the same song, reaching listeners from modern day stereo speakers produces a very different entertaining effect or quality than one reaching us from the earlier gramophone. The song or the message is the same, but the medium of delivery or the messenger is different. Thus the entertaining appeal of the song is greatly enhanced by the messenger. In the same vein a movie seen from a high definition modern day television screen has a much higher entertaining appeal than a television screen of earlier times.

In this way, some kind of fusion or indistinct aspect of the song or play exists with the medium of delivery. In other words, this fusion has resulted in what has been called a convergence of communication, between the creative act itself and the medium of delivery. Technologies like optic fiber, micro circuits, micro processors, distributed processing, systems engineering techniques, and very sophisticated software techniques are continually enhancing the entertaining quality of the creative product itself.

For example, as Viacom's chairman Mr. Redstone stated before the U.S. Senate Subcommittee on antitrust hearings(see appendix B), the trend into the future of entertainment points to one of high technology, ranging from encryption, compression, and transmission of signals to set-top boxes and delivery of programming. Technology is delivering a plethora of developments in the entertainment and information industry that would increase the choices available to the viewing public. Consumers will have more entertainment and wield more control over their entertainment services. The electronics and service platform will empower consumers to personalize their service and use tomorrow's television, for example, as a device to make their lives easier. However, due to the high financial resources or combination of skills and expertise that goes into building this information superhighway, as Telecommunications Incorporation's(TCI'S)chairman Mr. John Malone noted before the U.S. Senate Subcommittee on antitrust(see Appendix E), mergers and acquisitions will become an order in the industry. For example, as testified by John Malone, the cost to give existing cable and telephone networks the capability of carrying broadband, two-way interactive video programming and to equip subscribers to participate in these networks will run into at least $60 billion. The industry is a world of giant competitors where the ability to thrive calls for huge financial resources as well as high skills.

As Mr. Malone further noted in his testimony before the Subcommittee, this fast paced high technology is going to result in efficiency in society. The transportation of information at such break-neck pace will improve the efficiency of industries, thus enhancing productivity. Malone foresees, for example, efficient entertainment services where there will be video on demand, random access to any movie or television show whenever subscribers want to see them; video telephony, the ability to see friends and loved ones in very high quality at a very affordable price; broad-band telecommunications of all kinds; high-speed faxes, the ability to send and receive high-quality photographs in very short order, a very important feature in moving medical records around; multimedia applications and interactivity on client server basis.

Clearly, the sweeping technological changes going on in the telecommunications industry is not only going to benefit the entertainment industry, but also is going to affect all aspects of our lives. Whenever everything we do becomes easier and easier to do, surely, that is also entertainment. Of course seeing a loved one in poor health and suffering has a downside and nobody wants to see that. But being able to have your medical records moved around, or instead of going into the yellow pages and calling a doctor at random you are able to go in and see which doctors you can choose what their specialities are, and even see a video clip of doctors explaining their practice, their style of medicine you get some of the personality of the physician. That certainly brings some sense of relief and in that regard, it carries some entertainment quality because it brings some relief. This is one instance of what I meant by technology changing even the very definition of entertainment-through better information we get some measure of lift up, however, unpleasant. In the same vein, technology is aiding in tele-commuting, that is the ability of people to work at home instead of having to commute to a central location. Presently, a large workforce of customer service representatives exist that work out of their homes.

This enlarges employment to people who are handicapped. This brings relief to such employees, and it certainly has an entertaining quality to it, because anything that brings relief from the pressures and uncomfortabilities of life is, in a sense, entertainment.

We can go on and on with a list of those subtle branching outs that the path of entertainment is taking these days. For example, Personal Computers, inexpensive wireless communications are now abundant in the hands of people, ushering in the power of cellular telephony to the masses at affordable prices and no longer being an exclusive right of the wealthy. We are witnessing real-time feedbacks and all kinds of interactivity Probably the most beneficial and essential gains society will reap with these technological advancements is in education both in the classroom and at home. Interactive technologies will turn people from couch potatoes into full, participating students, in effect, in their homes and in the classrooms. It will be most entertaining for parents to be able to see what homework their children are getting, and be able to better assist with the education of their children. This is very crucial for society because, the fact is undeniable that education of the young is the bedrock of society

This paper is primarily intended for academia, where scientific observations are the norm rather than the exception. For this reason, this paper does not want to disgress into writings that may sound like Nostradamus, the fourteenth century French astrologer, in this discussion of the future of the entertainment and information industry. But discussion of any subject that deals with the future must, of necessity, involve some degree of conjecture because nobody really knows the future. In this regard, this paper cannot help but offer some unsubstantiated opinion while we are on the subject of education.

The primary objective of entertainment and information, I happen to believe, is to instruct and educate so as to help mold the behavior of members of society as to what is acceptable and what is not for the common good of all. If we would permit our imaginations to expand into the horizons, we could see that the much talked about dawning of the aquarian age, the age of information, the development of the sixth sense, and what Christians have called the return of Christ, the brotherhood of man is in fact what this technological advancement is shaping and bringing into the consciousness of the human race. For example, if radio waves can travel through space while lacking visible quality to the human eyes or ears, and technology can harness this energy to manifest on the television screen or the cellular phone, then surely this feat is enough to prod the thinking mind into inquiry. That, the human being is not just a limited particle or mote floating about in the universe. That, we must have some indeterminate essence part of us which you may choose to call a spark of divinity that does make us really interrelated and makes us all a part of the nous. Granted this premise, it is easy to see that as technological advancement permits education to become more and more accessible, we will more and more outgrow our ignorance and assume the real nature of 'God', with all its divine attributes of goodwill towards all human beings. When this condition of the human race's mind supervenes, the age of information, knowledge, maturity has arrived and the saying of antiquity that, "...they shall beat their swords into plowshares, and their spears into pruninghooks"[4] will begin to take more practical meaning for humankind. Again, this is not an attempt at discourse by this book on a topic lacking substantiation, but rather it will come about with more and more technological advancement. For example, a friend well known to this writer once commented that, if television had been invented earlier, the holocaust could have been prevented. What this friend probably meant to say was that the advent of television has now made the world a truly global village in that, as soon as violence or catastrophy rears its head anywhere in the world, the speed with which it is brought to international attention prevents its deterioration into the experiences of the holocaust. Such is the way the technological advancement will bring about the "beat[ing] [of] their swords into plowshares." But unfortunately, these ancient injunctions

---

[4]The Book of Isaiah 2:4, *The Bible.*

have been presented under a cloud of symbols and metaphors that lack practicality to any serious-minded individual. It is up to technology to unveil the practicality of this surreal images so that they may increasingly find a place in the realm of academics. Then, what Philip James Bailey said that, "let each man think himself an act of God [Nature], his mind a thought, his life a breadth of God [Nature]; and let each try, by great thoughts and good deeds, to show the most of Heaven [goodwill towards another] he hath in him," will find its practical meaning in society through technology.

So, as John Malone testified before the Senate Subcommittee, the great on-going strides by technology will lead to all kinds of interactive television, not just the kind of fun stuff, playing along with "Jeopardy" for small prizes, but for bigger and more important prizes beneficial to society, being able to react to Ross Perot when he poses the question of whether it is a dumb idea to have real-time democracy and real-time feedback.

Demanding Public

It appears that the stamina of the public for sticking out with entertainment products such as a screenplay or a song wears out faster these days. In other words, the public's interest in a new entertainment product wanes far more quickly than in earlier times. This condition may be the result of competition and the advancement in technology which are constantly introducing newer forms of product delivery and programming. This vast array of product delivery systems seems to be lowering the entertaining quality saturation point of the audience, or easily bores them. For example, you may hear a pleasing song on the radio today, but within a very short span, a newer song appears that seems to be more pleasing than previous one and instantly relegates the previous one to the background on the hit list. A similar thing happens with screenplays.

As mentioned at the outset of this book in Chapter I, there is a growing demand on the part of the public or the audience for a more elaborate and spectacular entertainment product. A movie with name stars and big special effects could easily run into $50 million. It appears that the impact of competition, technology and the demanding public interact on each other. Each is augmenting the effects of the other in bringing about this convergence in the entertainment and information industry. For example, competition may lead firms into the introduction of innovative products in order to stay in business. But without the know-how or technology, the introduction of these innovative products could be stalled. Then, once the product is introduced, the public insatiety for even better, elaborate, and spectacular products fans the cycle, leading to unending innovative products.

Conclusion

The future of the entertainment and information industry appears to be heading towards international expansion. It is going to see the use of various operating forms, such as, company-owned operations, joint ventures, and franchises for the different foreign markets. Even though, there is a strong universal nature of entertainment, companies may have to adjust their usual methods of carrying on business because local conditions often dictate a more appropriate method, and also because the operating forms used for international business differ somewhat from those used on a domestic level. For example, in the U.S. Walt Disney plans events at different times in order to stagger the hours when people use the restaurant facilities.

In Europe, the British are usually done with lunch before 1 p.m., when the French begin theirs; and the Italians and Spaniards arrive at about the time the French leave. Also typically, Europeans are not very enthusiastic about amusement parks; the adults find it trying to act like children for an entire day. They prefer other types of leisure outings, especially in winter, as evidenced by the fact that no European amusement park has made money by staying open year-round.[5] For example, although an estimated 88 percent of people in the U.S. and Canada visited an amusement park in 1991, only 18 percent of Western Europe did. As a consequence, several European theme parks, including Mirapolis, Magic Planet, and Zygofolies failed within five years of start-up.[6]

The industry, similar to other industries, is following the path of international business which, it is generally believed, has been growing recently at a faster pace than it did in earlier years, and also at a faster pace than domestic business has been recently. For example, in the early 1970s, less than 5 percent of U.S. production was sold abroad and approximately the same amount of U.S. total purchases were imported goods and services. Twenty years later, these figures had more than doubled, surpassing more than 10 percent each.[7] It appears the reasons firms go after international business, as mentioned earlier,-to expand sales, acquire resources, and to diversify sources of sales and supplies-would have applied in earlier times as well.

So, what are the causes in recent years that are bringing about the rise in international business? The answer can be found by going back to the factors we discussed earlier-expansion of technology, increase in global competition, and the demanding public. Perhaps, we might also add that development of supporting institutional arrangements also make globalization quite appealing. Much of what we now take for granted has resulted not only from expanding technology but also from the devel-

---

[5]John D. Daniels and Lee H. Radebaugh, *International Business: Environments and Operations*, 7th Ed., Addison-Wesley Publishing Company, 1995, New York, 6.

[6]Ibid., 7.

[7]Ibid., 11.

opment by businesses and governments of institutions that facilitate the effective application of that technology. Walt Disney can easily distribute films in foreign countries because of advances in transportation facilities as well as the evolution of various institutional arrangements that make trading easier. As an example, as soon as Disney's films arrive in French customs, a bank in Paris can collect the distribution fee, in francs, from the French distributor and then make payment to Walt Disney, in U.S. dollars, at a bank in the U.S.[8]

In contrast, if these supporting institutional arrangements were not in place, or were still being conducted as in the era of barter days, Disney probably would have to accept payment in the form of French merchandise, such as wine or perfume. The merchandise then would need to be shipped back to the U.S. and sold before Disney could realize any usable income.

Although, barter trading is still around, it is less common and not much popular due to its cumbersome, time-consuming, risky, and expensive nature. Business increasingly relies on the institutions that facilitate international trade, among them are banks, postal services, and insurance companies. Today, most exporters and importers receive or make payments for goods and services with relative ease, through instruments such as bank credit agreements, clearing arrangements that convert one county's currency into another's, and freight insurance underwritten by giant companies such as Lloyds that covers loss or damage en route and nonpayment by the buyer.

The future of the entertainment and the information industry, as rightfully noted by the two authorities of the industry, Mr. Sumner Redstone of Viacom Incorporation and

Mr. John Malone of Telecommunications Incorporation(see Appendices B and E), is one that is ever going to have intense competition

---

[8]John D. Daniels and Lee H. Radebaugh, *International Business: Environments and Operations*, 7th Ed., Addison-Wesley Publishing Company, 1995, New York, 6.

due to the dizzying pace of technology. For firms to stay competitive and remain in business dictates that they go after larger and larger markets.

That precisely is the case, as evidenced by Viacom's recent acquisition of CBS for $35 billion, Daimler Benz-Chrysler merger, and America On Line-Time Warner merger, all running into several billions of dollars. It appears that is going to be the trend of the twenty-first century well into the foreseeable future, a trend that seems to be obeying the dictates of doing business in this global village technology has wrought. With resources, especially financial so much limited, the necessary financial resources demanded by this industry can only be amassed by huge conglomerates, mergers, and acquisitions.

About the Author

The author holds a BS degree in international business from Mercy College, and an MBA degree in finance from the Long Island University. He had been a professional merchant marine officer for nearly a decade, and has traveled extensively throughout the world. A novelist as well, he enjoys writing, and currently has a book, *The Rugged Terrain to the American Dream*, available wherever fine books are sold. He resides in New York with his family.

Appendix

Appendix

Appendix A

HEARINGS

BEFORE THE

SUBCOMMITTEE EXAMINING THE EFFECTS OF MEGAMERGERS
IN THE TELECOMMUNICATIONS INDUSTRY

ON ANTITRUST,
MONOPOLIES AND BUSINESS RIGHTS

OF THE

COMMITTEE ON THE JUDICIARY UNITED STATES SENATE

ONE HUNDRED THIRD CONGRESS

FIRST SESSION

ON

EXAMINING THE EFFECTS OF CERTAIN MERGERS IN THE TELECOMMUNICA-
TIONS INDUSTRY ON COMPETITION AND INFLATION, FOCUSING ON THE
MERGER OF QVC NETWORK, INC., AND VIACOM, INC., FOR PARAMOUNT
COMMUNICATIONS, INC., AND THE MERGER OF TELE-COMMUNICATIONS,
INC., AND LIBERTY
MEDIA CORP. INTO BELL ATLANTIC CORP.

OCTOBER 27, NOVEMBER 16, AND DECEMBER 10, 1993

Serial NUMBERS J-103-33

U.S. GOVERNMENT PRINTING OFFICE
84-880 CC WASHINGTON: 1995
ISBN 0-16-046464-1
COMMITTEE ON THE JUDICIARY

JOSEPH R. BIDEN, JR., Delaware, Chairman

EDWARD M. KENNEDY, Massachusetts	ORRIN G. HATCH, Utah
HOWARD M. METZENBAUM, Ohio	STROM THURMOND, South Carolina
DENNIS DeCONCINI, Arizona	ALAN K. SIMPSON, Wyoming
PATRICK J. LEAHY, Vermont	CHARLES E. GRASSLEY, Iowa
HOWELL HEFLIN, Alabama	ARLEN SPECTER, Pennsylvania
PAUL SIMON, Illinois	HANK BROWN, Colorado
HERBERT KOHL, Wisconsin	WILLIAM S. COHEN, Maine
DIANNE FEINSTEIN, California	LARRY PRESSLER, South Dakota
CAROL MOSELEY-BRAUN, Illinois	

CYNTHIA C. HOGAN, Chief Counsel
CATHERINE M. RUSSELL, Staff Director
MARK R. DISLER, Minority Staff Director
SHARON PROST, Minority Chief Counsel

SUBCOMMITTEE ON ANTITRUST, MONOPOLIES AND BUSINESS RIGHTS

Howard M. Metzenbaum, Illinois, Chairman

DENNIS DeCONCINI, Arizona	ORRIN G. HATCH, Utah
HOWELL HEFLIN, Alabama	STROM THURMOND, South Carolina

PAUL SIMON, Illinois   ARLEN SPECTER, Pennsylvania

BILL CORR, Chief Counsel
THAD STROM, Minority Chief Counsel and Staff Director
**WILL TELECOMMUNICATIONS MEGAMERGERS
CHILL COMPETITION AND INFLATE PRICES?**

WEDNESDAY, OCTOBER 27, 1993

U.S. SENATE
SUBCOMMITTEE ON ANTITRUST, MONOPOLIES AND BUSINESS RIGHTS,
COMMITTEE ON THE JUDICIARY,
Washington, D.C.

The subcommittee met pursuant to notice, at 9:54 a.m., in room SD-226, Dirksen Senate Office Building, Hon. Howard M. Metzenbaum(chairman of the subcommittee)presiding.

Also present: Senators Simon, Hatch, Thurmond, and Specter.

OPENING STATEMENT OF HON. HOWARD M. METZENBAUM, A U.S. SENATOR
From the State of Ohio

Senator METZENBAUM. We will start this hearing a little early because there are two votes on the floor of the Senate. I will ask the first panel of witnesses to take their seats.

We are here today to begin a series of hearings on the wave of megamergers that are sweeping the telecommunications industry. Before any of these mergers are allowed to go forward, there is one overriding question that we must answer for the American consumer; that is, will this unprecedented convergence of telecommunications giants create a swarm of cost-cutting entrepreneurs of a handful of price-gouging monopolists. Before any telecommunications deal is approved by the antitrust authorities or the Federal Communications Commission, we in Congress must be able to assure the American people that we know the answer.

I have not made up my mind about any particular merger. However, I do have serious reservations about many of them, including Bell Atlantic's merger with Tele-Communications, Inc., QVC's merger with the Home Shopping Network, AT&T's acquisition of McCaw Cellular Communications, and the contest between QVC and Viacom to acquire Paramount. The subcommittee will hear more about these deals from Bell Atlantic, Viacom, and Paramount today. We have been in contact with TCI, QVC, and AT&T, and expect them to appear before the subcommittee at a future date.

I believe that some press accounts have oversimplified and even distorted my position on the complex issues involved in these mergers. Let me make my position clear today. I do not believe that a deal is necessarily good or bad because it is big. The concerns I have expressed about certain mergers are based on my reasoned judgment that consumers can be exploited by conglomerates that wield too much market power. The elimination of competition and the potential to compete is, in most instances, harmful to consumers. The key is excessive market power, not size alone.

To that end, I am frank to say that the deal that concerns me the most is the merger of Bell Atlantic with TCI. Together, these monopolists will form a colossus which will have a telephone or a cable wire connecting approximately 40 percent of the homes in America. As you can see by the chart to my right, this deal will also give the new conglomerate control of the lion's share of America's most popular cable programing. Frankly, I had planned to recite the entire list of TCI-controlled programming until I realized that it would add 5 to 10 minutes to this opening statement. Moreover, TCI can make a sizable addition to its stable of programming if QVC-in which TCI already owns a 28 percent stake-acquires the Home Shopping Network and Paramount.

Given the size and scope of Bell Atlantic's and TCI's holdings, the merger could create a megamonster. It would have formidable power to dominate the cable market and to freeze competition which would otherwise occur between local phone companies and cable television systems. Such a concentration of power cannot be dismissed lightly by the Congress, the antitrust authorities, or the Federal Communications Commission.

To my mind, the Bell Atlantic deal raises four fundamental questions. First, can the merger of two huge monopolies that would otherwise be fearsome rivals usher in greater competition? Second, should any restrictions be imposed on the new conglomerate's ability to leverage its power in the cable programming and distribution markets? Third, can FCC and State regulatory authorities governing phone and cable companies adequately protect consumers? Finally, is there anything unique about this combination of monopolists that cautions against the merger?

First, it is no secret on Wall Street that local telephone and cable monopolies were positioning themselves to compete against one another. Both Bell Atlantic and TCI have made public statements to that effect. At a March 1990 hearing before a House Energy and Commerce Subcommittee, one of Bell Atlantic's vice presidents stated that "Bell Atlantic wants to be a full-service cable company and was capable of competing with entrenched cable companies." Likewise, at a cable television public affairs forum in March 1992, John Malone of TCI stated that TCI would "look at new revenue opportunities such as *** residential phone service."

Now, the merger will put an end to any possibility of competition between Bell Atlantic and TCI, which is an issue that the antitrust authorities will have to consider. Gauging the anticompetitive effects of a merger that eliminates a potential rival is an issue that the antitrust laws have wrestled with for at least three decades. The Supreme Court clearly articulated this concern in its 1964 *Penn-Olin* decision stating that "The existence of an aggressive, well-equipped and well-financed corporation*** waiting anxiously to enter [a] market would be a substantial incentive to competition which cannot be underestimated."

Another antitrust issue is whether approving this deal could lead to an industry dominated by a handful of telecommunications conglomerates that have powerful incentives to coexist instead of compete. In antitrust terms, this is called mutual forbearance. The theory is that a conglomerate which is relatively strong in a particular market may refrain from competing aggressively with a conglomerate in another market out of fear of retaliation. Clearly, such a tacit agreement not to compete would harm consumers by inflating prices and limiting choices.

My second major concern about the deal is how much Bell Atlantic's financial deep pockets will entrench TCI's market power in the cable industry. That could raise new entry barriers against other phone companies or small entrepreneurs experimenting with new technologies. As it stands now, TCI has dominated the cable market shrewdly positioning itself as the industry's gatekeeper. It has done so by amassing an extensive array of cable programming and building a vast set of cable systems.

Let me explain. First, a cable system can't be successful if it doesn't have the programs that viewers demand, such as news , shows, movies, sporting events, and shopping channels. Currently, most of these programs are owned by the cable companies themselves. However, TCI owns or controls more programming than any of its competitors. That gives TCI the power to cripple its rivals and to keep new competitors out of the market by refusing to sell programming to them on reasonable terms.

I might add that Bell Atlantic is well aware of the barriers to entry that allowing one company to own so much programming creates. In a January 1993 filing with the FCC, Bell Atlantic stated that "Cable has used its control of programming to impede the development of competing distribution systems by denying access to cable-owned programming or by providing access on unfavorable, discriminatory terms."

Second, the reach of TCI's cable network allows it to control a rival programmer's access to the entire cable market. TCI has the Nation's largest cable television system. It reaches about 25 percent of all cable subscribers. The conventional wisdom in the industry is that a new cable program cannot break even unless it reaches the critical mass of viewers that subscribe to TCI's cable system. That means TCI's decision not to carry a program, for whatever reason, can doom it.

Bell Atlantic itself has acknowledged that cable systems have abused their power to control which programming gets to market. In a January 1993 filing with FCC, Bell Atlantic complained that "Cable operators have also impeded the development of independent programming sources by denying them access to their monopoly cable systems."

I expect the antitrust authorities to take a hard look at whether the new conglomerate has too much power to chill competition because of its market penetration and its control over so much cable programming.

My third major concern about the merger is whether regulatory measures are sufficient to control anticompetitive conduct in this industry. As we will hear from several of today's witnesses. Federal regulations have not prevented Bell Atlantic and TCI from using anticompetitive business tactics against their rivals in the past. I believe that is significant and should also be considered by the antitrust agencies.

I am aware that the Cable Act passed by the Congress last year prohibits a great deal of anticompetitive conduct. However, the new law has not been tested and may not be sufficient to curb all possible abuses of the new conglomerate's market power.

Bell Atlantic seems to share my general skepticism. It recently sued to have the FCC's decision on cable rates overturned in favor of regulations that would reduce cable rates by 28 percent. In its pleading, Bell Atlantic described the FCC's decision as "arbitrary and capricious." It also claimed that the FCC rules left cable rates "inflated" and permitted "monopoly operators to continue exercising market power control contrary to the congressional purpose."

I also have doubts about whether the new FCC rules can prevent cable and telephone conglomerates from making monopoly profits at the expense of consumers. Prior to the merger, Bell Atlantic expressed similar doubts. In a January 1993 FCC filing, it urged the FCC to regulate the cable industry to "ensure that cable operators do not evade the Commission's rate regulations by recovering monopoly profits through inflated prices."

In summary, it would be & mistake for the antitrust authorities to rely on untested administrative remedies to protect consumers from telecommunications conglomerates. Finally, I believe that we must be especially careful to scrutinize a merger that involves the medium through which our society communicates the basic values of our democratic society. The exchange of views on television, over the phone, and through computer networking would be influenced by a merger of this breadth.

Therefore, I want to be certain that our antitrust authorities scrutinize the broad political and social ramifications of this merger. As John Shenefield, the Carter administration's antitrust chief, stated almost 15 years ago in testimony before the subcommittee:

The relationship between economic size and political influence*** is a fairly direct one. People across this country*** [grow] quite concerned when they see a "limited number of corporate decision makers, in effect, governing their lives without direct responsibility, with no public mandate, and without any accountability."

It is altogether appropriate for the antitrust authorities to consider the pervasive power that a telecommunications conglomerate would have to influence our democratic institutions. I would also expect the antitrust authorities to take appropriate steps to block or modify this merger if, after careful scrutiny, the concerns that I and others, including State regulators, consumer groups, and the National Association Broadcasters have raised, persist. However, I am confident that the Department of Justice will pursue this merger with the vigor it deserves. Their statement indicates that "The proposed telecommunications acquisitions will be analyzed under all plausible theories of competitive harm."

At the conclusion of my statement, I will include in the record a statement submitted to us by Ms. Anne Bingaman, head of the Antitrust Division of the Department of Justice.

I intend to stay involved in this matter and to look carefully at other proposed mergers in this industry, and if I believe that it is necessary, I will propose legislation to adjust our communications policies in the phone and cable industries. I plan to work closely with my colleagues to review the 1992 Cable Act and the 1934 Communications Act to ensure that our antitrust and communications policies work in tandem to protect consumers from being victimized by telecommunications conglomerates.

Appendix B

TESTIMONY AND PREPARED STATEMENT OF
SUMNER M.REDSTONE
CHAIRMAN, VIACOM INCORPORATION

BEFORE THE

SUBCOMMITTEE ON ANTITRUST,
MONOPOLIES AND BUSINESS RIGHTS

OF THE

COMMITTEE ON THE JUDICIARY
UNITED STATES SENATE

ONE HUNDRED THIRD CONGRESS

Senator METZENBAUM: Mr. Redstone, we are delighted to have you with us this morning.

STATEMENT [TESTIMONY] OF SUMNER M. REDSTONE

Mr. REDSTONE: Thank you. Good morning, Mr. Chairman and members of the subcommittee. My name is Sumner Redstone and I am chairman of Viacom International, Inc. I really wish to thank the members of the subcommittee for this opportunity to testify and humbly to commend the chairman and the members of the subcommittee for their consideration of issues now which will affect the telecommunications industry for decades to come, and possibly to avoid a catastrophe.

While the subcommittee has a variety of issues to consider, I will speak to three areas of particular concern to Viacom, and more importantly to the American public. First, I will discuss the structural problems in the cable industry today caused by the extraordinary and abusive monopoly power wielded by TCI.

Second, I will describe why any enhancement of that market power will further choke competition, specifically why TCI's bid through QVC Network for Paramount Communications, as well as the proposed merger of Bell Atlantic and TCI/Liberty, will have cumulative, significant anticompetitive effects.

Third, I will outline the basic elements of Viacom's strategic vision for the communications industry and explain the procompetitive effects and consumer benefits of the Viacom/Paramount merger.

Over the last several years, TCI-and this is no overstatement-has been the bane of the American cable industry and the American cable consumer. Through a complex web of TCI companies, TCI has systematically attempted to exert monopoly power over almost every aspect of the cable industry. Today, TCI-controlled cable systems control exclusive access to well over 20 percent of American cable homes, and together with its partners and would-be partners in QVC, Comcast, Cox, and Newhouse, TCI controls access to one in every three such homes.

TCI's exclusive access gives it the power to make or break independent programming services-and it does-because given the need to reach a critical mass of cable subscribers, a programming service that is not carried by TCI-controlled cable systems has little or no chance to survive. As a result, TCI can and does extract onerous conditions to carriage, often obtaining an equity interest in otherwise independent programming services.

In our particular case, TCI and Liberty have threatened to deny carriage of our premium services, Showtime and The Movie Channel, and have refused to renew affiliation agreements for that carriage. TCI has also threatened, and I quote, to "crucify" The Movie Channel by dropping it from TCI's systems in favor of Liberty's own Encore service. These threats were designed to force Showtime Networks into a low-ball merger with Encore and to weaken or eliminate Showtime Network's competitive position.

There are many examples of this kind of activity that do not involve our company. In other examples of TCI's predatory conduct, which may be found in my written statement, TCI/Liberty, one, insisted that NBC change the focus of its cable network, CNBC, in order to prevent competition with TCI-controlled Turner Broadcasting's CNN, prompting then Senator Gore, now Vice President Gore, to call the incident, and I quote, a "shakedown by TCI."

TCI and Liberty extracted an equity interest in Court TV by threatening to create a cloned service and refusing to carry Court TV on TCI's cable system. TCI chilled the bidding for The Learning Channel. All it did was say, you can buy it, but if you do, it is off TCI's system. The result was that TCI ultimately purchased The Learning Channel for $20 million less than the original bidder, Lifetime, in which we have an interest, offered to pay.

Significantly, in addition to its dominance in cable distribution, TCI and Liberty now own all or part of at least 25 cable programming services in the United States. TCI has also set out to control various technological developments, from encryption, compression, and transmission of signals, to set-top boxes and delivery of programming to homes, again leveraging its market power over access to American cable subscribers for its own benefit.

This, together with TCI authorization center, a facility that will employ proprietary technology to encrypt, digitally compress, transmit, and control signals from individual programming services-in effect, TCI seeks control not only over content, but over carriage. This will enable TCI to use new technology to create new bottlenecks in the distribution of cable programming services.

The net result of TCI's predatory practices is that TCI typically demands lower license fees from unaffiliated programmers and extracts monopoly rents in the form of higher prices from consumers. As TCI drives down the wholesale price it pays unaffiliated programmers, such programmers will cut back on what they spend on programming. Program diversity, so essential to the principles of our Constitution and quality, are sacrificed.

Our dealings with TCI, our personal dealings in which I have been personally involved, have proven one economic fact of life. TCI's dominant position in cable distribution nationwide when coupled with its vertical integration into programming, creates intolerable monopoly power. I don't know of a single industry in the United States today where that kind of power exists or is exercised.

Several weeks ago after suffering, along with other cable programmers, at the hands of TCI for years, we took TCI to court, seeking substantial damages for their monopolistic and predatory practices, and we are also challenging TCI's latest attempt to injure our business, a merger that was worked on for 4 years, a consensual merger, through its bid through QVC to upset the strategic merger with Paramount.

TCI's acquisition through QVC of Paramount can only aggravate the serious structural problems I have described. To understand the very real danger of a Paramount acquisition by TCI/QVC, one must understand the level of vertical integration and program protection that TCI has already achieved.

Turner Broadcasting, which is substantially controlled by TCI, has acquired, or will soon acquire, control of independent studios New Line and Castle Rock. TCI has also entered into agreements providing for a substantial equity interest in Carolco Pictures, and according to published reports TCI is looking at deals with MCA's Universal Studios and Sony's Columbia and Tri-Star Pictures.

Should TCI/QVC acquire Paramount, TCI will have significantly enhanced power to dictate terms to programmers, threatening that, unless such programmers accept TCI's terms, TCI will replace their programming with programming produced by its captive studios. By depressing to below-market levels the rate of return of unaffiliated programmers, program diversity, and quality will suffer. TCI now pays us nothing to carry VH-1. We could complain. They could drop VH-1 and VH-1 is out of business.

TCI and its partners' market power is dangerous enough, but when coupled with the publishing, television, and motion picture production and other interests of Paramount, the dangers to fundamental first amendment principles designed to further diversity of voices, multiplicity of viewpoints, and freedom of access to the marketplace of ideas, are sobering. This is especially significant in the light of the threatened combination of two of the largest publishers, something that hasn't been focused on, in the world, Paramount and Newhouse, another partner of TCI. This combination would create the single largest and most powerful publisher, presenting in and of itself serious antitrust questions.

As I said, this combination would create the single largest and most powerful publisher, presenting in and of itself substantial antitrust questions with respect to our control of communications in a household. Its superhighway is really an exclusive toll road which we believe will impose content-based charges on those who wish to communicate through it.

Unlike TCI and Bell Atlantic, Viacom favors a truly open telecommunications superhighway, ensuring everyone an equal chance to step up to the microphone. That superhighway should be content-and identity-neutral, and Congress should require that superhighway to be a two-way operating system that is entirely open.

What we have here is a combination of two great monopolists. We have all heard for years how monopoly will lower prices and advantage the consumer, but this has never happened. What we have here is the elimination of two potential competitors.

In contrast to the acquisition by TCI/QVC of Paramount and the proposed Bell Atlantic/TCI merger, Paramount Viacom will combine two companies with different yet complementary strengths. Rather than entrenching an abusive monopolist, Paramount Viacom will create a new, strong competitor, in which each partner can build on each other's programming expertise and talent.

The emergence of Paramount Viacom is particularly important to assure America's traditional worldwide leadership in the creation of programming. Viacom is already an international leader in marketing its programming services all over the world. It has, in effect, created through MTV the first international global network.

Paramount Viacom will have an even greater ability to create and export programming with broad international appeal and enhance American competition worldwide. Paramount Viacom will also provide direct and almost immediate benefits to American consumers, such as the creation of America's first true interactive educational television network for kids, drawing on Simon & Schuster for its educational publishing expertise and on Viacom and its Neckelodeon unit for their expertise in children's programming and interactive media.

In conclusion, the situation facing us today is not at all unlike that of the old Bell System. The difference here is that the anticompetitive effects can be avoided in the first instance without waiting for the disaster to assume full form before remedial measures are taken.

TCI has monopoly power now and exploits it. Think about this. TCI right now reaches 20 percent of cable subscribers in the United States. With its partners, it reaches one in every three homes in the United States. With Bell Atlantic, it will reach approximately 50 percent of consumers in the United States. Leaving aside all issues of abuse of power, that kind of power should not be lodged in any one company or in any one man.

PREPARED STATEMENT OF SUMNER M. REDSTONE

SUMMARY

1. Today, TCI-controlled cable systems are gatekeepers, controlling exclusive access to well over 20 percent of American cable homes. That exclusive access gives TCI monopsony power to "make or break" independent programming services, because given the need to reach a critical mass of cable subscribers, a programming service that is not carried by TCI-controlled cable systems has little or no chance of commercial success. If the Bell Atlantic TCI/Liberty deal is completed, TCI will have access to one in every two American homes, enhancing TCI's already prodigious "make or break" power.

2. TCI has been able to leverage its dominant access to American cable homes into cable programming. As a result, TCI and Liberty now own all or part of at least 25 cable programming services in the United States. TCI thus has the power(through its dominant access to cable homes)and the incentive(through its ownership of programming services. And, if TCI acquires Paramount(through QVC), TCI will have even less need for independent programming. As a result, creativity will be stifled, program quality will be diminished and cable service prices to consumers will rise.

3. TCI has also leveraged its market power to obtain control over critical technological developments, including encryption, digital compression, transmission and set-top box access to the home. Given the bottlenecks that TCI has already created in the delivery of cable services, we fear letting the same people build and control the coming communications "superhighway."

4. The TCI/QVC/Paramount transaction, by virtue of TCI's market power and the market power of TCI's partners and would-be partners in QVC, raises serious antitrust questions in itself. The Bell Atlantic/TCI/Liberty combination will only make a bad situation worse. If either proposed combination is allowed to proceed, the American

consumer will be forced to pay more for lower quality programming and less diversity in programming. We urge the government to take the time to understand and deal thoroughly with these issues before allowing either combination to proceed. Without government intervention now, it will be much harder to fix the structural problems later-and it may well be impossible to compensate consumers for the harm they will suffer in the interim.

Good morning, Mr. Chairman and Members of the Subcommittee. My name is Sumner Redstone and I am the Chairman of Viacom International Inc. I wish to thank the members of the Subcommittee for the opportunity to appear at today's hearing.

As I am sure you know, Viacom International Inc. is a diversified entertainment and communications company, which employs approximately 5,000 people worldwide. At the core of our company is Viacom Networks, which consists of MTV Networks and Showtime Networks Inc. MTV Networks includes three advertiser-supported, basic cable television networks: MTV: Music Television; VH-1/Video Hits One and Nickelodeon/Nick at Nite. Showtime Networks Inc. operates three premium television networks: Showtime, The Movie Channel and FLIX. We are also joint owners of Comedy Central, Lifetime and All News Channel-three additional advertiser-supported, basic cable networks. Our cable division owns and operates cable television systems that serve approximately 1.1 million customers. Our broadcast division owns five television and fourteen radio stations. Through our entertainment division, we produce programs for the broadcast networks and for first-run syndication. Our new media group is working to develop, produce, distribute and market interactive programming for the stand-alone multimedia and interactive market place which is fast emerging.

In light of recent developments in the communications industry, the work of this Subcommittee, as well as that of federal, state and local regulators and others charged with shaping and enforcing communications policy, is immensely important. We are witnessing the dawn of a new age of communications, a revolution every bit as profound as Bell's invention of the telephone.

As with the development of our nation's telephone system, we should expect enormous technological advances in this communications revolution. But, also as with the development of the telephone system, the future communications system is susceptible to the leveraging of market power and other anticompetitive practices by those who dominate the nation's local delivery systems. The time for decisive action to ensure free competition and the full benefits of the communications revolution is now, and not, as with old Bell system, years from now when the anticompetitive effects are manifest. Without the vigilance of Congress, the Federal Communications Commission and the antitrust enforcement agencies, the American public will be denied many of the advantages the communications revolution otherwise would bring.

This revolution is happening at a breakneck pace. If these changes hurtle past policy makers without appreciation of their potential anticompetitive implications, it will take at least a decade of reform-regulation, public enforcement and private litigation-to remedy the situation and, in the meantime, American consumers will be the victims, rather than the beneficiaries, of technological innovation. If allowed to proceed unchecked, the risk is that consumers will suffer as creativity is stifled, program quality is diminished and cable service prices rise. What is at stake is nothing less than the way that Americans will receive information, communicate with one another, and interact-well into the next century.

While the Subcommittee has much work and a variety of issues to consider, I will confine my remarks to three areas of particular concern to Viacom and, I believe, to the American public. First, I will discuss certain structural problems in the cable industry today, caused by the extraordinary-and abusive-monopoly power wielded by Tele-Communications Inc.("TCI")and the companies it controls. Second, based on our experience in the cable industry, I will describe why any enhancement of that market power, indeed TCI's stranglehold, in the communications industry-specifically, the proposed merger of Bell Atlantic and TCI and TCI's affiliated company, Liberty Media Corp.("Liberty")and TCI's bid, through QVC Network, Inc.("QVC"), for Paramount Communications Inc.("Paramount")-will further choke competition and lead to a closed communications "superhighway" built and ultimately controlled by TCI and those affiliated with it. Third, and finally, I will outline the basic elements of Viacom's strategic vision for the communications industry, and explain the procompetitive effects and benefits to consumers of the proposed merger of Viacom and Paramount.

1. TCI'S MONOPOLISTIC AND PREDATORY POWER IN THE AMERICAN CABLE INDUSTRY

Over the last several years, TCI has been the bane of the cable industry and the American cable consumer. Through a complex web of companies it controls or influences, TCI has systematically attempted to exert monopoly power over almost every aspect of the cable industry and, most recently, the technological developments that are the key to the future of our industry.

Today, TCI-controlled cable systems are gatekeepers, controlling access to well over 20 percent of American scale homes. No other cable operator comes close to that size. Even Time Warner(the second largest scale operator in the United States)controls access to only half that number of homes, and the next group of cable operators are one-fourth TCI's size. And together with its partners and would-be partners in QVC-Comcast, Cox Enterprises and Newhouse-TCI controls access to one in every three American cable households. With the addition of the Bell Atlantic service base, TCI and those affiliated with it will have access to one in every two households-creating overwhelming power. By contrast, Viacom's cable system holdings are de minimis(about one-twelfth the size of TCI), and provide service to less than two percent of all cable subscribers in the United States.

To understand the source and extent of TCI's dominance, one must understand the unique characteristics of the cable industry. TCI's level of exclusive access gives it the power to make or break cable programming services, among other things, as it sees fit. Unlike any other industry that comes to mind, the cable industry is unique in that even a 20 percent market share could result in such monopoly power.

TCI's "make or break" power derives from the fact that to successfully launch and operate a national cable programming service, that service must reach a sufficient base or "critical mass" of subscribers in order to generate sufficient advertising revenues or subscriber fees. In the case of a nationwide advertiser-supported basic cable programming service, such as Viacom's MTV and Nickelodeon, the "critical mass" of subscribers required to succeed is roughly 40 million of the current 57 million available subscribers. Premium television services, such as Viacom's Showtime and The Movie Channel, have extraordinarily high fixed costs, and therefore are also heavily dependent on wide distribution by cable operators in order to amortize those fixed costs. Further, in the case of premium services, wide distribution by cable operators is not enough. Premium services, where carried, also need to be favorably marketed by cable operators(including favorable positioning, packaging and retail pricing)in order to encourage consumer subscriptions to individual services. Due to TCI's control of well over 20 percent of cable would require that service, at a minimum, be carried by nearly every other cable system in the United States for it to succeed commercially-an impossible hurdle to overcome.

TCI also wields its market power in subtle-but no less anticompetitive-ways. Our experiences has shown that TCI attempts to leverage its market power over access to American cable subscribers in order to lighten its grip on programming services and other aspects of the cable industry. TCI often dictates grossly unfair terms as a condition to carriage of programming services. As to existing programming services, TCI often threatens to deny carriage, refuses to renew affiliation agreements and threatens to drop programming services entirely, knowing that without access to TCI's systems, programming services cannot succeed.

In our case, TCI and Liberty have threatened to deny carriage on their cable systems of our premium television services-Showtime and The Movie Channel-and have refused to renew affiliation agreements with Showtime Networks for carriage of those premium services. TCI has also threatened to "crucify" The Movie Channel by dropping it from TCI's cable systems in favor of Liberty's own Encore service.

These threats were designed to force Showtime Networks into a low-ball merger with Liberty-owned Encore Media and to weaken or eliminate Showtime Networks' competitive position. These tactics are part of a pattern by TCI to extract an equity interest in third-party programming services. For example, TCI used its monopoly muscle to buy The Learning Channel when it was put up for sale. Lifetime(a joint venture of ABC/Capital Cities, Hearst and Viacom)submitted a bid for The Learning Channel of $50 million, while TCI offered only $30 million and ultimately withdrawn. TCI then purchased The Learning Channel for $30 million.

In another example of TCI's power to eliminate programming competition, when NBC began to develop its own all news cable network, the Consumer News and Business Channel, CNBC, TCI pressured NBC into changing the focus of CNBC in order to prevent competition with TCI controlled-Turner Broadcasting's Cable News Network. According to then Senator, and now Vice President, Gore, TCI kept CNBC off the air until TCI was assured that CNBC would not compete with CNN. Vice President Gore called the CNBC situation a "shakedown by TCI."

In the case of start-up programming services launched by third parties, TCI uses a similar tactic-threatening to create a clone of the new programming service, which TCI threatens will be carried on TCI's cable systems in lieu of the third party's new service, if TCI's demands for an equity interest in that service are not met. Because carriage on TCI's systems is essential for a new service to succeed, TCI's demands for equity tend to be met. For example, we understand that Liberty extracted an equity interest in Court TV in just that way-threatening to create a clone service and refusing to carry Court TV on TCI's cable systems. Afraid of losing its sunk costs, Court TV gave in to TCI and today, Liberty owns thirty-three percent of Court TV.

TCI(and Liberty)now own all or part of at least 25 cable programming services in the United States(including Encore, QVC Network, Home Shopping Network, Superstation WTBS, CNN, Headline News, TNT, The Cartoon Channel, The Family Channel, The Discovery Channel, Sportschannel America, X*Press Executive and The Box).

TCI has also set out to control various technological developments-from encryption, compression and transmission of signals to set-top boxes and delivery of programming to the home-again leveraging its market power over access to American cable subscribers for its own benefit. TCI has created bottlenecks which give it control of the delivery of programming by cable and satellite, including control of encryption and compression technology. This, together with the construction of the TCI Authorization Center-a facility that will employ proprietary technology, as TCI sees fit, to encrypt, digitally compress, transmit and control signals from individual program services-will enable TCI to use new technology to create new bottlenecks in the distribution of cable programming services. TCI thus will be able to further leverage its existing monopoly power by refusing to distribute any programming not transmitted through the TCI Authorization Center.

The net result of TCI's predatory practices is borne by cable programmers and the American consumer alike: TCI typically demands lower license fees from programmers in which TCI has no equity interest and extracts monopoly rents(in the form of higher prices)from consumers that will sacrifice diversity, choice, quality and creativity in cable programming. Why? As TCI drives down the wholesale price it pays to such unaffiliated programmers, those programmers will have to cut back on what they spend to create programming. As TCI knows, those programmers have no other viable way to get their programming to cable consumers in TCI's franchise areas except through TCI, so they must accept TCI's terms. Because TCI attempts to-and often does-deny unaffiliated programmers a fair return on their investment, those programers will spend less, program quality will deteriorate and-most importantly-viewers will suffer. Thus, TCI will continue to rob the marketplace of the incentive to create better television, and consumers will be the losers.

In contrast to TCI's typical practice of paying unaffiliated programmers license fees which are substantially below market rates, we believe that TCI frequently pays programming services in which it or Liberty has an equity interest full license fees. In these cases, TCI increases not only artificially low license fees payable to its competition, but creates artificially high license fees for its own affiliated programming services. The benefit to TCI of this is twofold, first, TCI is able to leverage non-TCI cable systems into paying those high license fees for its own affiliated programming services by demanding the same license fees that TCI itself pays, and second, TCI is able to depress the license fees payable to its competition because non-TCI cable systems frequently refuse to pay license fees for non-TCI programming which are higher than the license fees paid by TCI for such non-TCI programming. The effect overall is an increase in consumer prices for cable services and a diminution in program quality and choice.

Because of our success in creating programming with broad consumer appeal, Viacom has been a thorn in TCI's side. Perhaps because we have attempted to resist its efforts to leverage its existing market power, TCI has targeted us for its most egregious forms of conduct. Among other things, TCI has tried to acquire Showtime Networks on unfair terms; attempted to destroy The Movie Channel for the benefit of TCI/Liberty's own premium movie services; and acquired studio production capabilities through TCI-related companies and entered into exclusive motion picture output agreements, at predatory prices, for TCI/Liberty's own premium movie services, in order to deny Showtime Networks access to that motion picture output. TCI is willing to overpay for the right to this output since TCI will be recompensed through the monopoly tax TCI will then charge American consumers in the form of higher prices for cable television.

Several weeks ago, after taking TCI on for years in the marketplace, we took TCI to court. We have sued a number of TCI-controlled companies, including Liberty and QVC, in New York federal court seeking substantial damages for their monopolistic and predatory practices. We are also challenging TCI's latest attempt to injure our business-its bid, through QVC, to upset our strategic merger with Paramount. At bottom, our dealings with TCI have proven one economic fact of life: a dominant position in cable distribution nationwide, when coupled with vertical integration into programming, creates intolerable monopoly power; TCI has it, and it uses it. I therefore believe that TCI's market power must be addressed immediately; I also believe that, if the past is prologue, TCI's latest attempt to control the coming communications "superhighway" must be stopped. We simply cannot afford to wait until TCI's closed superhighway is in place, and then spend the next ten or more years trying to open it.

2. A BELL ATLANTIC WILL ONLY MAKE A BAD SITUATION WORSE

The combination of Bell Atlantic and TCI can only aggravate the serious structural problems that are the source of the anticompetitive power that TCI so brazenly abuses. The primary reason-and primary danger-is that when TCI's, its partners' and would-be partners' share of U.S. cable homes are combined with Bell Atlantic's share of the local telephone service business, estimated to be in excess of 17 percent, the combined entity will be able to reach into virtually 50 percent of American homes. TCI already abuses its control of its local cable franchises, and if allowed to merge with Bell Atlantic, the new combination will possess overwhelming power which can only exacerbate the kind of anticompetitive conduct in which the current TCI already engages. There is simply no question that kind of power should not be concentrated in one company.

If completed, the proposed merger between Bell Atlantic and TCI will give Bell Atlantic /TCI/Liberty an entrenched dominant presence in 48 of the 50 states and in 59 of the top 100 U.S. local markets. This massive combination will control access to 22 million telephone and cable customers-without taking into account the market power and reach of TCI's partners and would-be partners in QVC. If TCI sought to acquire each of the cable systems it does not already own located in the Bell Atlantic service areas, antitrust enforcers would surely view the attempted acquisition as having grave anticompetitive consequences, and the FCC would prohibit that acquisition as a blatant violation of the FCC's horizontal ownership well in excess of the FCC's limits-although TCI tries to gloss over it by the use of superhighway rhetoric.

TCI has already engaged in a series of corporate shell games, essentially shuffling assets in order to avoid the strictures of federal regulation. One need look no further than the history of TCI and Liberty to predict the future. When threatened by restrictions on vertical integration and horizontal concentration, TCI "spun off" Liberty, with majority voting control ending up in the hands of John Malone. And now that the danger from those regulations has apparently been avoided, Liberty and TCI have announced that they will recombine, with the financial benefits of that recombination flowing to TCI/Liberty's controlling shareholder, John Malone.

This makes one suspicious that the same pattern will undoubtedly be followed in the Bell Atlantic/TCI deal. The companies have announced that if they fail to obtain regulatory approval allowing TCI's cable franchises and Bell Atlantic's local telephone service to operate in the same geographical areas, those cable assets will be "spun off" in order to "solve" the problem. However, as in the TCI/Liberty spin-off, the assets will go to none other than the stockholders of TCI/Liberty and their controlling shareholder, John Malone. The regulations will be satisfied on their face while their underlying purpose will be subverted. Control will still lie with TCI through common ownership and interlocking directories.

TCI has also long used hardball tactics with local governments to get its way. When the small town of Morganton, North Carolina, concluded that TCI's service was "atrocious" and decided not to renew TCI's cable franchise, the Mayor, Mel Cohen, began to explore building a municipal cable system. In response, TCI declared war on the project and on Mayor Cohen. TCI sued the town for $35 million, hired a lobbying firm to propose a referendum giving TCI a lifetime franchise, and ran negative ads to defeat Mayor Cohen's reelection. TCI spent upwards of $140,00 on the campaign, in contrast to the $600 spent by the incumbent. The town fought the lawsuit and won, and the Mayor was reelected, but TCI has continued to appeal the ruling. While the case is on appeal, TCI retains the cable franchise and its $1.3 million annual proceeds. Indeed, in a familiar tactic, TCI offered to sell the system to a consortium of buyers, but the town refused to approve the sale when it discovered that one of the purchasers was owned and controlled y TCI. In a similar, and no less telling story when a dispute arose between the town of Vail, Colorado and TCI over rising rates and poor service, over one weekend TCI exhibited nothing but the home phone numbers of the mayor and the city manager.

With that history in mind, the new, bigger TCI with its enhanced market power, will be ale to step up its destruction of anyone who does not play by TCI's rules. TCI already successfully dictates terms of carriage to almost every programmer, and Showtime Networks, which is fighting for its very survival against TCI's anticompetitive tactics, is living proof of that power. And if past is prologue-and it is-TCI will use this power to favor its own programming as well as to extract ownership interests and unreasonable low license fees from unaffiliated programming services.

TCI proposes illusory cures for these serious concerns. First, publicly TCI promises a better tomorrow with plenty of competition. Meanwhile, privately TCI so thoroughly dictates economic conditions today in the cable industry that competition tomorrow will be far too late to control TCI's abuses. The situation is not unlike that of the old Bell system. The difference here is that the anticompetitive effects can be avoided in the first instance, without waiting for the disaster to assume full form before measures are taken to remedy the situation. TCI has monopoly power now and exploits it now. The acquisition by TCI, through QVC, of Paramount will only further enhance TCI's monopoly power and its ability to abuse it. The Bell Atlantic deal will only make things worse, and no amount of rhetoric from TCI or Bell Atlantic will change that inevitable fact.

3. DIFFERENCE IN VISIONS FOR THE DATA SUPERHIGHWAY

How is the Viacom/Paramount merger-with the recently announced investment in Viacom by NYNEX Corporation-different from TCI's proposed Bell Atlantic/TCI/Liberty combination? Aside from very important structural differences(which I will get to in a moment), there is a fundamental difference in our vision of the way people will communicate.

TCI has spent a lot of time lately talking about the Bell Atlantic deal as the fulfillment of the long-awaited electronic superhighway. But TCI speaks out of both sides of its mouth. While promising an open highway and free competition-using buzzwords like "connectivity," "system compatibility," and "open architecture"-TCI has also boasted that the Bell Atlantic/TCI combination "will allow us to control all of the communications needs of a household with one device." Similarly, Raymond Smith, Chairman and CEO of Bell Atlantic, has stated:

Our fundamental strategy is very straightforward Number one, to de develop a full-service network capable of delivering voice and data and image and video using both wired and wireless technologies in high-growth markets, both domestically and internationally. Number two, to develop the information, entertainment, and transactional services that can be offered over that network. And number three, to develop operating systems that allow customers easy access to those services.

Thus, while Bell Atlantic and TCI have promised that the proposed merger will bring "choice, control and convenience in the communications marketplace," what this really means is TCI's choice, TCI's control and TCI's convenience. But, as they say-and as TCI itself recognizes-the devil is in the detail, and TCI and Bell Atlantic are providing no detail. They are saying, in essence, "trust us, we will do the right thing." They cannot be trusted, however, and their vision is not of a truly open, content-neutral, superhighway, where any programmer has unimpeded access to viewers on commercially reasonable terms.

Viacom favors this type of truly open telecommunications superhighway, supporting both competition and First Amendment values, and ensuring everyone an equal chance to step up to the microphone. We believe the superhighway should be content and identity neutral. What that means is that as in an actual highway, a toll is paid to gain access to the highway and that toll is not determined by what a particular vehicle is carrying or the owner of that vehicle. An empty truck owned by company "A" pays the same toll as one owned by company "B" whose truck is loaded with goods worth a million dollars. The toll taker collects tolls based on volume of usage, not the value of goods carried or the owner of the truck. In other words, as with the telephone system today, people should pay based on how much they use the superhighway, not what they say or do on it or who they are.

What TCI has not told you is that its superhighway is really an exclusive toll road which detours competition and which we believe will impose content-based charges on those who wish to communicate through it. It is not the road to the future but a path to a past of unchecked monopolies and arbitrary censorship. As both Bell Atlantic and TCI have made clear, their superhighway will give them full control over the programming from its point of origin through its delivery to the home. And they mean to levy tolls on both programmers and consumers at several points along the journey.

The first toll booth on TCI's superhighway will collect a fee imposed on users of the superhighway for initial access, and that fee will not be a flat rate, but rather will be levied on a sliding scale based on TCI's perception of the value of the particular programming. The second toll booth will collect the fee TCI will charge to exit the highway and unlock the key inside the set-top box TCI has placed there, in order to access the viewer. And the third, and most pernicious, toll booth will be the one that collects the charge for obtaining the specifications to the operating system that will control the interactive lanes of the highway, without which programmers will be unable to create software capable of accessing the highway.

By manipulating crucial technologies over which it has the ability to gain control, we believe that TCI will control what the set-top box is allowed to receive or not receive. Already TCI's market power has made its choice of set-top box the de facto industry standard. By the same token, Bell Atlantic/TCI will select the proprietary technology and equipment necessary to construct their superhighway, and given the fat that their superhighway will be the first constructed and capable of accessing virtually 50 percent of all American homes, it is safe to assume that the Bell Atlantic/TCI superhighway operating system will also become the de facto industry standard. If this occurs, Bell Atlantic/TCI's control over the technology of program delivery, and thus over programming itself, will be almost absolute.

We need to be sure that TCI's superhighway is more than just a means to detour both competition and free speech. To that end, I suggest that you ask TCI a few questions about just what TCI means by an "open" superhighway. Because of TCI's vagueness and its use of politically correct buzzwords, it may be impossible to pin TCI down, or ask all the right questions. Nevertheless, we would begin with the following:

1. *Will TCI charges be based strictly on the amount of usage of the superhighway?* In other words, TCI should charge for the number of trucks on the road, but not for the subjective value it places upon their cargo.

2. *Will TCI divest its entire interest in programming to a wholly unrelated third party?* Such a sale will help to prevent the threat of discrimination against non-TCI programmers' access to TCI's highway.

3. *If not, will TCI limit its affiliated programmers' use of its highway to no more than a specific percentage of the highway's total traffic capacity?* TCI has spoken of the virtually unlimited capacity of TCI's highway. But in actuality, capacity can be limited in a manner designed to permit TCI to continue to discriminate against unaffiliated programmers by reserving a large portion of limited highway capacity for its favorite sons. A specific percentage cap on its usage will help ensure that TCI builds the highway as penly as it promised.

4. *Will TCI subscribe to standardized, non-proprietary data formats(e.g., MPEG II for video and Dolby AC-3 for audio?)*And will TCI agree not to place a proprietary transport layer on its data signal? In other words, will it make the highway usable by all vehicle makes and models?

5. *Will TCI's highway and set-top boxes support the use of at least two encryption processes?* Such a move will promote both signal security(by offering redundancy in the event that one encryption process is compromised)as well as competition.

6. *Will TCI permit the set-top boxes to be sold as a commodity(like telephones are now-but were not always), whereby all manufacturers have open access to the necessary technology and specifications to build compatible equipment and which all programmers can access?* Or will it force a household that wants to get other programming services to go to the expense of getting another set-top box? In effect, this would be no different from forcing a family to buy multiple television sets simply to access different channels.

7. *Will TCI operate its Authorization Center as a non-profit free trade zone?* In other words, will TCI allow programmers to sell their services directly to the viewer(or to other cable systems or other distributors), or will it insist that its Authorization Center serve as a gatekeeper which directly controls whether a consumer receives a given service?

After you pose these questions to TCI, the more vague assurances or "don't know's" you hear, the more worried you should be. All that I ask is that you do not put the highwayman in charge of the highway. Viacom believes that, at a minimum, Congress should require that the superhighway be a full, two-way operating system that is entirely and truly open, and further, that the software specifications for access to the superhighway be made publicly available.

4. TCI'S ACQUISITION OF PARAMOUNT WOULD FURTHER STIFLE COMPETITION AND CREATIVITY IN THE CABLE INDUSTRY.

If Paramount falls to TCI, through its controlled company, QVC, it will be further able to control not only the method and manner of non-broadcast access to a critical mass of American homes, but it will be further able to exclude from the marketplace or competitively disadvantage any programming provider who will not agree to its terms, and replace that provider's programming with TCI's own program offerings. The result of TCI's exclusionary tactics has been and will be to inflate prices to consumers, reduce quality and deny adequate returns for third-party programming, the supply of innovative television.

To understand the full context and the very real danger of a Paramount acquisition by TCI/QVC, one must understand the vertical integration TCI has already achieved. For example, Turner Broadcasting, which is substantially controlled by TCI, has acquired, or will soon acquire, control of independent studios New Line Cinema and Castle Rock Entertainment. TCI has also entered into agreements providing for a substantial equity interest in Carolco Pictures. And, according to public reports, in addition to its intent to acquire Paramount, TCI is considering deals with both MCA's Universal Studios and Sony's Columbia Pictures and Tri-Star Pictures.

What are the dangers of TCI controlling Paramount? Once TCI has Paramount, TCI will have the enhanced power to dictate terms to Viacom and other programmers by wielding the threat that unless such programmers agree to its terms, TCI will replace their programming with that produced by its captive studios. By diversity depressing to below-market levels the rate of return of unaffiliated programmers, quality, and new sources of programming will be thwarted to the detriment of the

American viewing public. Indeed, the power that TCI would have to control programming and cable distribution is dangerous enough by itself, but when coupled with the publishing, television, and motion picture production and other interests of Paramount, the danger to fundamental First Amendment principles designed to further a diversity of voices, a multiplicity of viewpoints and freedom of access to the threatened combination of two of the largest publishers in the world, Paramount and Newhouse. This combination would create the single largest and most powerful publisher, resenting, in and of itself, substantial antitrust questions. If TCI's plans are fulfilled, it will be TCI which determines which voices, viewpoints and ideas are carried on the nation's superhighway. Indeed, TCI could end up controlling the news we receive and the content of our children's schoolbooks.

DIFFERENCES IN VIACOM'S ACQUISITION OF PARAMOUNT

As I mentioned earlier, there are obvious and meaningful differences between the proposed Bell Atlantic/TCI/Liberty combination and NYNEX's investment in Viacom. Most fundamentally, Bell Atlantic and TCI are merging their entire operations. Two companies which would otherwise compete in an expanded marketplace are becoming one, thereby eliminating the benefits of that competition. In contrast, NYNEX's relationship with Viacom is completely different, since the two companies will remain operationally independent. NYNEX'S is simply making a passive investment in Viacom and NYNEX's will have no right to control Viacom's actions or vice-versa. Any future coordination between NYNEX and Viacom will occur only as a result of arms-length negotiations between independent parties for the benefit of two separate shareholder constituencies. Bell Atlantic/TCI/Liberty will combine to create one gigantic $60 billion company which serves only one shareholder constituency, whose largest shareholder will be John Malone.

In contrast to the proposed Bell Atlantic/TCI merger, which simply makes the nation's biggest cable operator even bigger, the proposed Paramount Viacom International will combine two companies with different-yet complementary-strengths. Rather than entrenching an abusive monopolist, Paramount Viacom will create a new, strong competitor in which each partner has access to and can build on each other's programming, expertise and talent, the very embodiment of First Amendment values.

The emergence of Paramount Viacom International is particularly important to ensure America's traditional worldwide leadership in the creation of programming. Viacom is already an international leader in marketing its programming services to Europe, Latin America and Asia. Paramount Viacom International will be a company with an even greater ability to create and export programming with broad international appeal and thus enhance American competition worldwide.

The proposed Paramount/Viacom merger will do far more than help the U.S. balance of payments. It will provide direct and almost immediate benefits to American consumers. For example, Paramount's Simon & Schuster, the leader in educational publishing, will be able to tap into Viacom's expertise in interactive television technology and together will create many new consumer offerings, such as a new Nickelodeon designed as the first, true interactive educational network for students of all ages and disciplines.

Conclusion

In conclusion, I appreciate your commitment to ensuring a fair and competitive environment and to the principles of freedom of expression that you have long labored to guarantee every American. I thank you and will, of course, be happy to answer any questions you may have.

Appendix C

STATEMENT OF MARTIN S. DAVIS, CHAIRMAN AND CHIEF EXECUTIVE
OFFICER, PARAMOUNT COMMUNICATIONS, INC.

BEFORE THE

SUBCOMMITTEE ON ANTITRUST,
MONOPOLIES AND BUSINESS RIGHTS

OF THE

COMMITTEE ON THE JUDICIARY
UNITED STATES SENATE

ONE HUNDRED THIRD CONGRESS

Senator METZENBAUM: Thank you very much, Mr. Redstone, Mr. Martin Davis, chairman of the board and chief executive officer of Paramount Communications, we are happy to hear from you, sir.

Statement Of Martin S. Davis

Mr. DAVIS: Thank you. Mr. Chairman and members of the subcommittee, good morning. My purpose today is to tell you why the Paramount Communications board voted unanimously to enter into a merger agreement with Viacom, a decision we announced on September 12, 1993.

We are proceeding with this merger agreement on the basis of a revised and enhanced offer to our shareholders just made by Viacom, an offer which, we strongly believe, provides our shareholders with more value, both short and long term, more than the unsolicited hostile takeover bid announced by QVC.

Let me now turn to the basis of our agreement with Viacom. Paramount is a copyright-driven, American-owned enterprise. Our operations are primarily in film and television production, as well as book publishing. Our studio in Los Angeles, I might add, was founded in 1912. Today, we are one of the Nation's leading publishers of educational textbooks and related instructional materials, as well as a premier trade book publisher through Simon & Schuster.

Paramount operates the now completely modernized Madison Square Garden and its popular regional sports cable network, five recently acquired and expanding theme parks, and seven UHF broadcast stations. Paramount also helped to launch USA and SciFi, two successful cable networks jointly owned by MCA.

Over the past decade, the worlds of entertainment and publishing, our two core operations, were forever altered by changes sweeping through our marketplace both here and abroad. These dramatic changes posed formidable challenges to our management and, if I may, let me cite some of them.

First, aided by a weak dollar and by less rigorous foreign accounting practices, European and Japanese companies have entered the U.S. market on a massive scale. Foreign owners are now in control of large Hollywood studios and have gained an enormous beachhead for the production of films, television and cable programming, as well as access to valuable film libraries. They have also acquired a number of major American publishing houses who produce instructional materials for our schools.

Second, our competition overseas has intensified as we pursue new global opportunities in the information and entertainment fields. Our competition now comes in large measure from horizontally and vertically integrated, foreign-owned entities who are protected and shielded by their governments in a trade playing field which is far from level when it comes to American companies. If the United States is to remain a robust competitor in Asia and throughout the Common Market, then only those American companies with strong complementary product franchises and efficient distribution systems will succeed over the long run.

Third, within our own country the media lineup has been radically transformed. Companies that were once independent and limited to a single market have joined forces across the product and service lines, as well as technologies, to create powerful multinational and domestic giants against whom we must also compete.

On that note, what must be of concern to you as members of the Antitrust Subcommittee, as it is to us as independent programmers, is the extraordinary market power amassed by the cable forces who are an integral part of the QVC lineup.

First, we have TCI, which is by far the Nation's largest cable operator, with over 10 million subscribers. Add to that the 3-million-plus subscribers in Liberty Media, soon to be folded back up again by John Malone into TCI. But it does not stop there. Comcast, part of the original QVC group, has 2.6 million subscribers, making it the fourth largest cable operator. The more recent QVC allies are Cox Cable, with 1.7 million subscribers, and Newhouse Cable, with 1.3 million, the fifth and seventh largest MSO's. This brings the grand total to nearly 19 million subscribers. Effectively, this nationwide cable cartel would give TCI and its partners the ability to control access to one out of every three cable homes in America. When you throw in the Bell Atlantic service area, it is frightening to contemplate that the TCI/QVC group would hold the power to control the cable gateway to one out of every two homes in this country.

This concentration of market power does not even stop there. The TCI/Liberty Malone empire owns all or part of as many as 23 cable networks and 16 regional sports networks. This combination of horizontal and vertical power would have an even greater anticompetitive mass if it were to succeed in acquiring the Paramount Studio, as well as controlling the MSG Cable Network and or 50-percent interest in USA Network.

A QVC-Paramount board consisting of TCI, Liberty Media, Comcast, Newhouse, and Cox nominated directors would exert enormous leverage over the marketplace not only in cable, but in publishing, since Newhouse's Random House competes head to head with Simon & Schuster.

Surely, this aggregation of media power in so few hands must somehow be brought under control if we are to preserve the values of competition, programming diversity, and the best interests of the consumer. Our antitrust agencies must take a long and hard look at the anticompetitive aspects of the QVC hostile takeover bid for Paramount.

May I give you some historical perspective with a direct bearing on the subject before you. During the 1930's and 1940's, companies who owned the movie seats also owned the movies that were being shown. This combination of content and carriage was stifling competition and hurting the consumer.

In 1948, our Government broke up this vertically integrated monopoly in, as it turns out, the Paramount case. Despite the handwrringing at the time, the hand-wringing film makers prospered. They were able to increase their production not only to serve their traditional market, the theaters, but the new, free television markets which were then opening up. I submit that we are in the same situation today. Instead of movie seats, there are armchairs in the living room in front of a screen in the form of a television set wired for cable.

Question: By severing the link between the cable program ownership and the control over the means of delivery, could we, by taking a leaf out of the Paramount case book, serve both the consumer and increase competition in this new media age? The new media gateway, I submit, whether it is called the communications superhighway or whatever label one chooses to affix, must be open to all programmers on a fair and equitable basis.

Despite the intent of the 1992 Cable Act, a crucial question you must answer is whether large, integrated cable combines like TCI will be able to continue to discriminate against independent cable programmers by denying them fair access to their delivery systems. By so doing, they can block the only currently available cable media path to the customer. These cable bridge-keepers should no longer be allowed to hold up independent program drivers by charging exorbitant tolls or by keeping them off the cable roadway.

In the face of the structural changes in our business environment that I referred to earlier, it became clear to management that Paramount could not simply stand pat. Since I became chairman of Paramount in 1933-a company that at that time was known as Gulf+ Western where I have spent almost all of my working life-my colleagues and I began to explore a number of alternative directions. These strategies were aimed at equipping Paramount to become a first-class competitor in the domestic and international arenas, and thus to build long term rather than short-term shareholder values.

A decade ago, we redefined our businesses by sharpening our focus on entertainment and publishing. We were not afraid to undertake the challenge of deconglomerating and to concentrate on what we considered to be the growth areas of the future as the information age began to dawn. In so doing, we created exciting opportunities for the writers, editors, directors, producers, and performers, the talent that is at the heart of our business. And we did so while strengthening our balance sheet by paying down our once very heavy debt load and increasing our liquidity. In the process, our shareholder values increased ten-fold.

During this restructuring, we also began to explore the possibilities of a business combination to find, if you will, an ideal fit. In pursuing that course, we wanted to avoid the dangers of highly leveraged or bust-up transactions that undermined so many companies in the "go for it" eighties. Our strategy led us to a careful search for an acquisition that could meet these criteria: first a compatible management culture and business philosophy; a combination that would present no antitrust hurdles-we believe in competition, not in the heavy hand of monopoly: a financially strong association without the need to sell off valuable assets, dislocating employees and their families as well as the communities in which they live; a creative and innovative product mix, proven entertainment franchises, and a motivated talent base together with a global distribution and marketing system, taking full advantage of the latest delivery technologies; and most importantly, a community of interest that would enable us to grow and build our business together for the long haul, businesses that would inform, entertain, and educate audiences both here and around the world.

Viacom's chairman, Sumner Redstone, and I have been business associates since the mid-1950's when he built a successful film exhibition circuit throughout New England. Over the past 4 years, Sumner Redstone and I talked about the possibilities of a Paramount-Viacom merger. Last summer, these spirited and arms length negotiations gained momentum. They culminated in the friendly merger agreement approved by the Paramount board. Clearly, I am convinced our agreement with Viacom meets all of the criteria I outlined. Together, our combined companies can achieve more and compete more vigorously than each could have done in its own right.

We saw a commitment to maintaining the integrity of our assets and a resulting company that would accelerate its growth, expand employment opportunities, and promote the flow of exports-the uniqueness and popularity of American intellectual property that can measurably improve the U.S. trade balance.

Senator METZENBAUM. Can you wind up, please?

Mr. DAVIS. Pardon?

Mr. DAVIS. I am almost there, sir.

We could not identify any antitrust or regulatory problems. In fact, we are pleased to note that our proposed merger with Viacom last week received the required Hart-Scott-Rodino approval from the U.S. Government.

Finally, we recognize that Paramount Viacom, while still only half the size of Time Warner and smaller than Fox' News Corp. or Sony-Columbia, Matsushita's MCA or the German Bertelsmann Group, could serve as a model for a new form of business alliance, one prepared to meet the global goals of competition, programming diversity, and state-of-the-art product innovation, while at the same time honoring our joint commitment to building long-range shareholder values.

Mr. Chairman, that completes my remarks. I am pleased to respond to your questions.

Appendix D

STATEMENT OF BARRY DILLER, CHAIRMAN AND CHIEF
EXECUTIVE OFFICER, QVC NETWORK, INC.

BEFORE THE

SUBCOMMITTEE ON ANTITRUST,
MONOPOLIES AND BUSINESS RIGHTS

OF THE

COMMITTEE ON THE JUDICIARY
UNITED STATES SENATE

ONE HUNDRED THIRD CONGRESS

Senator METZENBAUM. Thank you very much.
Mr. DILLER, we are happy to have you with us this morning, please proceed.

Senator THURMOND. Mr. Diller, I have another engagement. How long is your statement? I don't want to rush you, I just want to find out whether I will have time to ask some questions after your statement.

Mr. DILLER. Hopefully, it is brief. It shouldn't be more than a few minutes.

Senator THURMOND. Thank you. Proceed.

STATEMENT OF BARRY DILLER, CHAIRMAND AND CHIEF EXECUTIVE OFFICER, QVC NETWORK, INC.

Mr. DILLER. Good morning, Mr. Chairman, Senator Thurmond. Thank you for inviting me to speak on behalf of QVC and about the future of electronic retailing and about interactivity. QVC is a pioneer in the business of selling goods through a television set. In 7 short years, we have grown to over $1 billion in sales and we employ over 6,600 people in 6 states.

Over the past year, there has been enormous hype about the coming revolution in communications technology. I am wary of grand predictions. No one knows exactly when the information superhighway will be up and operational. One thing I do believe is that technological advancements are soon going to bring about a fundamental shift in consumer behavior.

Today at QVC, and every day, we answer over 120,000 phone calls. We deliver 85,000 packages. It may be a primitive first step into the world of interactivity, but it is real and it is growing. From the comfort of home, consumers tune us in, gather information, pick up their phones and order. Sixty percent of the people who try QVC become repeat customers. We have 4 million of them and we have won their trust because we offer consistent value and convenience. But I believe that electronic retailing is just the start of this process. For us, it is the fuel to make investments in laying down the technological tracks for the future.

As you know, I come from the world of what you might call pure entertainment. When I left Fox about 2 years ago, I spent 10 months learning about the growing flexibility and sophistication of telecommunications. I began to get a hunch that away from Hollywood and Manhattan, the pace was quickening; that the technological possibilities had come to a critical and practical mass; that there finally might be this convergence between computers, television sets, and a pipe thick enough to carry huge loads of information.

That is when I came upon QVC. There, I saw the first commercial application of interactivity, how and offer and response, simple and direct interactivity, was already happening. I knew then and I strongly still believe that QVC can play a central role in the architecture and development of this so-called information superhighway.

Connecting consumers to this pipeline of the future is obviously a daunting and wildly complicated task. To build the information superhighway will necessitate linkages and relationships in telephone and computers-working partnerships with content producers, which brings me to Paramount.

Our goal, stated at the outset, is to be a multimedia company, to expand beyond retailing into communications and entertainment and use our systems and technology to be the bridge in the architecture of this new world. QVC, along with our partners, Comcast, BellSouth, Cox Enterprises, and Advance Publications, will soon develop the expertise to deliver all kinds of goods and services to customers, not just camcorders and clothing, but entertainment, sporting events, and all kinds of educational and information products. Paramount's great store house of content will be crucial to such an undertaking.

As you are well aware, there are many companies that share similar hopes for the future. The list is endless and the race is on. I believe the competition will be fierce. Some will go it alone, others will form alliances. In our case, we chose cable and telco partners in a symmetrical balance because we believe both have much to contribute to a universe that we think will be nonexclusive and competitive.

But we may be wrong. Other configurations may win. Whatever happens, we believe that there are real opportunities for consumers and for companies. Some will succeed. Some, of course, will fail, but the benefit from all this frenzy will insure to the American people, who are going to get out of all this true and endless diversity in communications and entertainment. As for us at QVC, we can't wait to start.

Thank you.

Senator METZENBAUM. Thank you very much, Mr. Diller. Normally, the Chair would proceed at this point, but Senator Thurmond has to leave and I think he has some questions. Please proceed.

Senator THURMOND. Thank you, Mr. Chairman. Mr. Diller, you were willing to enter into a consent decree with the Federal Trade Commission to resolve quickly the antitrust issues raised by the involvement of TCI and Liberty Media in your bid for Paramount. Without revealing any strategy or details which should be kept confidential, do you see any other potential antitrust problems which could not be worked out to permit QVC's bid for Paramount to proceed on the merits?

Mr. DILLER. Senator, we did enter a consent decree.

Senator THURMOND. Speak into your microphone so we can hear you, please.

Mr. DILLER. We did not enter into a consent decree. Liberty Media did, and all antitrust approvals for our transaction have already gotten preliminary clearance. So we don't believe that there would be future regulatory issues.

Senator THURMOND. Mr. Diller, from your perspective, is the backing by NYNEX of Viacom's bid for Paramount significantly different from BellSouth's backing of QVC's bid?

Mr. DILLER. Well, it is different in the respect that BellSouth in its QVC investment will have full representation on the board and the economics are slightly different, but I think that is really the only area in which there is a difference.

Senator THURMOND. Mr. Diller, do you think it is likely that many cable companies could begin offering local exchange or other telephone services without the support of a telephone company?

Mr. DILLER. Yes, I do. I do believe that what is going to happen is that there is now going to be the chance, at least in video services, and I think also in telephony, but certainly in video services where you have a real opportunity to have two wires. The use of word "wires" now is so antique, but two wires, two competitive services I do think will have the opportunity to be banging against each other over the next 5, 10, 15 years. That will be the first time that there has been competition on anything other than over-the-air television; i.e., multiple services delivered by more than one provider, and I think that is healthy. I do think that competition is going to come from cable interests. It might come from telco-cable interests, but it will certainly come from some cable interests.

Senator METZENBAUM. Mr. Diller, we are pleased to have you with us.

Mr. DILLER. Thank you.

Senator METZENBAUM. I guess you are really entitled to congratulations. You had a battle in the courts and you won in the courts. I don't know if it has gone on to the court of appeals or whether the matter is completed. Is it completed or it is in the court of appeals?

Mr. DILLER. No, no. The supreme court, which is the senior jurisdiction, has upheld the lower court and that is it as far as the court is concerned. But winning is not just winning in court, though it does help.

Senator Metzenbaum. You at least won the first inning.

Mr. DILLER. We weren't knocked out.

Senator METZENBAUm. You got on first base. Now, the question is to get around to home.

Mr. DILLER. We weren't sent home.

Senator METZENBAUM. The QVC Network, which you chair, is engaged in a bidding war with Viacom for Paramount. In order to raise the nearly $10 billion that you needed to make a competitive bid for Paramount, you have had to strike a couple of different alliances. Initially, your bid for Paramount was backed by TCI and its spin-off company Liberty Media. As you know, that deal ran into anti-trust problems.

In a consent degree with TCI and Liberty Media, the FTC charged that allowing TCI to acquire any more cable programming would have been anticompetitive, and I agree with them. However, I must admit that I was surprised TCI dropped out of the deal so quickly and agreed to sell of its holdings in QVC. QVC was involved in the negotiations leading up to the FTC consent decree. Can you tell me why TCI abandoned the Paramount deal so quickly and what, if anything, TCI gained by dropping out of the deal, and are there any side understandings between you and Mr. Malone or any of his people?

Mr. DILLER. When John Malone made his announcement just previous to announcing his agreement with Bell Atlantic, and we talked about it, it became apparent that there might be additional regulatory issues by virtue of that proposed merger. He at that time said to me, I want you to know I will give you my word that we will stand aside; we don't want to stand aside. We have been in this with you since the beginning and since the beginning we have talked about the potential for acquiring Paramount, but I recognize that we may be a burden to this and so we will stand aside.

When he spoke earlier and you pressed him about the consent decree, I can tell you this. We were not a direct party to it, but I know that this was not something that Liberty wished to do. He did it and affirmed, redeemed, his pledge to me, which is that he would not stand in our way, and it was very clear that if that did not happen on the day that it happened, we would have been technologically knocked out of bidding for Paramount.

The only agreement other than the disposition of his shares that we entered into was one that would guarantee us to some degree-I shouldn't say that word overly strongly, but that would give Paramount and QVC access to the distribution that TCI had for cable for our products, and services, which was obviously very important to us. There was no other condition in the agreement.

Senator METZENBAUM. I am sure that the antitrust problems were recognized early on in the matter. Do I understand you to say that Mr.Malone came to you and indicated voluntarily that they would drop out?

Mr. DILLER. No; this was subsequent to the Bell Atlantic announcement. At that time, obviously there was much more attention on all of this. God knows that there wasn't a lot to begin with, but at that time when issues had been raised, I mean just in the air, he said that he would not stand in our way, and he kept his word and it was not an easy process to go through. I am obviously grateful for him doing so. They were under enormous pressure over a 24-hour period when it all came together to get that agreement signed-pressure brought by us, unfortunately, in this case. I mean, we had no other choice because of the fact that we literally would have been technically disqualified.

Senator METZENBAUM. You have some understanding with him as far as the TCI network continuing to carry QVC?

Mr. DILLER. Yes.

Senator Metzenbaum. I gather that was important to you because of their being such a major factor in the cable industry.

Mr. DILLER. They have a lot of distribution.

Senator METZENBAUM. On November 10, a few days before TCI dropped out of the Paramount deal, you questioned whether Paramount would have a problem getting distribution if it were acquired otherwise, otherwise meaning not by TCI and QVC. Your question suggests that any cable programmer that isn't owned or affiliated with TCI can face serious problems finding enough cable systems to distribute its programming. Can you tell me why you believe that Paramount would have problems being distributed if it is purchased by someone other than you or TCI?

Mr. DILLER. Certainly, I don't know whereof I ever made that statement about Paramount not being able to get distribution without a TCI affiliation.

Senator METZENBAUM. I have it as a quote, "Paramount would have a problem getting distribution if it were acquired otherwise."

Mr. DILLER. I can't imagine what I was referring to. I think that Paramount actually has the USA Network which it half owns with MCA which is distributed in as many homes as any other cable program service in the United States. QVC has got distribution assured for its products, or for its services, so I can't imagine what I was referring to.

Senator METZENBAUM. This is from Randall Mikelson: "Diller Sees More Options than Paramount," and it is a Reuters story. "Diller said, it is not a problem for me. The issue is would Paramount have a problem getting distribution if it were acquired otherwise."

Mr. DILLER. Maybe I was speaking about Paramount's proposed fifth network, but as I say, I don't know to what I might have been referring at that time. This getting on to be like the 100 Years War, so I don't know when that was written.

Senator METZENBAUM. It had to be somewhere around November

Mr. Diller. I honestly do not know what it refers to. I mean, clearly, distribution is a critical issue for people who have program services, but in the context of this particular quote I just don't get it.

Senator METZENBAUM. We won't make a big deal out of it.

QVC how has new partners in its bid for Paramount. You have allied yourself with three cable systems-Cox, Comcast and Newhouse-and BellSouth. You must think that the new bidding alliance won't run into the same antitrust problems that you had with TCI. As you know, I have publicly indicated that I have concerns that deals between telephone and cable companies will affect future competition between these two industries. Therefore, I have urged the antitrust agencies to look very closely at them.

Have you filed the BellSouth deal with the antitrust agencies for their review, and if not, when will you do so?

Mr. DILLER. We have already filed and we have received a preliminary clearance from the FTC. This is not a deal, however, between telcos and cable companies. This is a deal which involves a telco, BellSouth, and a series of cable companies making an investment in essentially a program producer. In that transaction, there are no edges given to any of the partners in terms of programming other than that they will have full access, but they get no special rights.

The issue for a program producer is, of course, to have the most avenues in which to sell his product. I believe that is coming in any event, and I think that if we are successful in getting Paramount the symmetrical relationship between our partners, I think, will be enormously helpful for us, but I can't see any anticompetitive effect.

Senator METZENBAUm. Well, I was interested in your statement that you had a preliminary review and clearance. Would you tell me how that came about?

Mr. DILLER. Well, BellSouth filed for making its investment in QVC, which received-I think it was at FTC rather than Justice-HSR clearance, and that took place some weeks ago.

Senator METZENBAUM. But that is before the Paramount deal came into the picture.

Mr. DILLER. No

Senator METZENBAUM. We won't make a big deal out of it.

QVC now has new partners in its bid for Paramount. You have allied yourself with three cable systems-Cox, Comcast, and Newhouse-and BellSouth. You must think that the new bidding alliance won't run into the sae antitrust problems that you had with TCI. As you know, I have publicly indicated that I have concerns that deals between telephone and cable companies will affect future competition between these two industries. Therefore, I have urged the antitrust agencies to link very closely at them.

Have you filed the BellSouth deal with the antitrust agencies for their review, and if not, when will you do so?

Mr. DILLER. We have already filed and we have received a preliminary clearance from the FTC. This is not a deal, however, between telcos, BellSouth, and a series of cable companies making an investment in essentially a program producer. In that transaction, there are no edges given to any of the partners in terms of programming other than that they will have full access, but they get no special rights.

The issue for a program producer is, of course, to have the most avenues in which to sell his product. I believe that is coming in any event, and I think that if we are successful in getting Paramount the symmetrical relationship between our partners, I think, will be enormously helpful for us, but I can't see any anticompetitive effect.

Senator METZENBAUM. Well, I was interested in your statement that you had a preliminary review and clearance. Would you tell me how that came about?

Mr. DILLER. Well, BellSouth filed for making its investment in QVC, which received-I think it was at FTC rather than Justice-HSR clearance, and that took place some weeks ago.

Senator METZENBAUM. But that is before the Paramount deal came into the picture.

Mr. DILLER. No, no, no. That was in contemplation of the Paramount transaction. Their investment in QVC is subject to the Paramount transaction being completed, and the filings attendant to it only contemplated that. BellSouth has an option beyond that to invest in QVC, if it chooses to do so, any time within the next 6 months if there is no Paramount transaction.

Senator METZENBAUM. I must confess that I am taken by surprise because I had not heard that occurred, and it would seem to me for them to have made a preliminary clearance-

Mr. DILLER. There are MFJ issues relative to BellSouth's making the direct investment in QVC, and those will be dealt with over a period of time. They have to clear all of the MFJ issues, but that is a separate-that does not relate to antitrust clearance. Now, you know, you go much further into this and you will soar over my head.

Senator METZENBAUM. Well, let me tell you why I am concerned about the antitrust aspects of your new bid for Paramount. The cable companies in your deal serve some of the largest markets in BellSouth's service area, such as Miami, FL: Charlotte, NC; and Charleston, SC. Time Warner, another major cable system in the area, already owns a 9-percent equity stake in your company. It seems to me that these cable companies and BellSouth could lose their enthusiasm for aggressive head-to-head competition if they are allowed to acquire a common interest in lucrative cable programming through your Paramount deal.

I expect immediately after this hearing to inquire of the FTC as to how this came aboutso promptly that clearance was given to BellSouth to go forward with the deal because it seems to me that it has some of the same problems about it that the TCI-Bell Atlantic deal has in it. But I don't see that being a question for you because you are really only a side player on that. It is between BellSouth and the governmental agencies.

Mr. DILLER. Well, it is true, it is not direct, but I reiterate that the transaction for Paramount is not a combination of telcos and cable in terms of offering services. It is an investment in a company where in the areas where they both provide service one of the key issues was would access be provided to both players. For instance, if BellSouth and Comcast compete in a market and Paramount has a service to offer, will they both be able to get it because they both intend to compete for it?

An issue here was, of course, the issue of nonexclusivity. Paramount-QVC-it is presumptuous for me to speak as if the transaction were completed, much though I wish it would be. The issue for Paramount is to sell its products to as many people as possible, bidding as high as they can bid. I fully expect that Comcast and BellSouth will be in situations where they will competitively bid up the product of Paramount.

The advantage to them in this transaction is that the product cannot be shut out from them. They will obtain at least access to it if, and only if, that is the sway of the business because it is possible the business will go into a world of exclusivity at some point.

The issue, of course, for Paramount or any program producer is to be fully competitive with the other people in their business who make programs because if they are not competitive, then they won't be in business very long. So nobody can ever get a distribution edge on a product for a content producer and thing they are going to stay in business happily for a very long period of time.

Senator METZENBAUM. Well, I would tell you-excuse me. I am sorry, Senator. Forgive me.

Senator METZENBAUM. That is all right.

Mr. DILLER. BellSouth's business is going to remain its business. This is going to be an investment for BellSouth. They are partner of ours in this, but they have a direct business. So, too, does Comcast.

Senator METZENBAUM. What percentage would BellSouth have in the Paramount deal?

Mr. DILLER. 12.5 percent.

Senator DILLER. Comcast is in its own business. QVC represents an investment for them. I promise you that where their own business is concerned, they will fight like crazy to keep competitive, not withstanding anything Paramount wishes to do. As a matter of fact, Paramount or any program provider could conceivably be caught in some way between those acts of competition, but the way it is going to get caught is if there are two bidders.

For the first time, I do believe that if the prohibitions against telcos providing video service in their own market are dropped, I think you will get two big, fat wires into the home, and I think that is going to be great for everybody. That has not happened in terms of multiple services, obviously, in a very, very long time.

Senator METZENBAUM. Prior to the Paramount deal, you had planned to merge with Home Shopping Network. As you know, I wrote to both the Antitrust Division and the FTC because I had serious concerns that consumers would be harmed by that merger. However, I now understand that you have dropped those merger negotiations. Do you have any plans to reopen those talks?

Mr. DILLER. No, we don't have any plans. We do not have any plans to reopen the discussions.

Senator METZENBAUM. I am curious as to what else QVC would expect to expand into. I don't watch the QVC channel that often. I am not really in the market for diamond rings or some kinds of rings that are being sold.

Mr. DILLER. We sell a lot more than that, Senator.

Senator METZENBAUM. I am sure that you do.(Laughter.)I am sure you do-amethysts and this and that, whatever-necklaces. It seems to me every time I turn it on-

Mr. DILLER. We sold 1,000 IBM computers at $1,100 a piece a couple of months ago.

Senator METZENBAUM. Congratulations, am I am not faulting you.

Mr. DILLER. Try wearing that around-well, excuse me.(Laughter.)Forgive me. I couldn't help it.

Senator METZENBAUM. You are taking me right down the road that I am interested in.

Mr. DILLER. Sorry

Senator METZENBAUM. Are there any limits as to what cable network shopping may have? In other words, is there a time when you may be selling sugar and various kinds of products not probably as expensive, but perhaps home consumer products of that kind?

Mr. DILLER. I think that the category is at its very beginning. I mean, QVC is here in this world of retailing. Electronic retailing is a $2-billion-plus business. Retailing is, what, half a trillion, or more. There is no structural impediment, I think, to QVC's growth because for convenience it is awful hard to compete with buying something from your home. I mean, I keep saying buying underwear in your underwear is hard to beat. We don't have investments in bricks and mortar, so it is very hard to compete with us on price because our investment relative to hard bricks-and-mortar retailers is so small.

In terms of information, I think you know you go to a store and you ask somebody to tell you about this and the[y] say, well, I just got here yesterday; I don't even know what it is, much less can I explain it to you. In 15 minutes today on a, for instance, photography show on QVC, you will learn more about how to operate camcorder than I think you will in almost any store that you can find.

So, I think that the ability, as QVC evolves out of its history of predominantly selling jewelry into offering all sorts of goods and services-I think that the opportunities are unlimited. I think that when you get a big, thick pipe with the ability to have huge servers and stored enormous amounts of video, you can sit at home and say I want every blue tie there is that looks like this or looks like that, and it will download to you and then it will be in your house 24 hours later.

I think that it is at the beginning of its process. It is a very, very immature business that has just started to grow and, as I said, I think that structurally there are no impediments to what it delivers.

Senator METZENBAUM. Would it be pretty difficult for a third competitor to get into the field?

Mr. DILLER. No; as a matter of fact, there have been a series of announcements recently. Time Warner and Spiegel have announced that they are starting a competitive home shopping service. Macy's has announced that they are. There have been a plethora of people who have made announcements that they are going to start home shopping businesses.

Senator METZENBAUM. As a matter of fact, I have a 1991 analysis of the home shopping market by the investment firm of Firm and Sells that states that the transpositions of QVC and HSN, combined with high barriers to entry, make it very difficult for new entrants to compete effectively with QVC and HSN. The barriers to entry identified in the analysis include large, fixed overheads and the difficulty a new entrant would face in getting its program distributed by cable companies.

Has anything about the home shopping market changed since 1991 to make it any easier for a new company to get in the market and be successful?

Mr. DILLER. Well, I think there may be some slightly more channel capacity. It is obviously clear that Macy's doesn't agree with that report. I mean, they have made a serious investment here. Time Warner also must not agree with it. They and Spiegel are spending, I would say, a considerable amount of money to get into the business. They must feel that they can get access to subscribers, and they must also feel that it is worth the candle.

Senator METZENBAUM. Mr. Diller, I am now reading from something given to me by one of my very able staffers. It says that I think you are mistaken about BellSouth's-

Mr. DILLER. As a matter of fact, I am, too. It says here in this little note here that they may not have gotten FTC clearance because their initial-I think I was not correct. I just assumed, because Advance did and Cox did in their transaction, that BellSouth did as well. But BellSouth's initial investment in QVC is as a loan, and the reason for that is because of the MFJ issues that need to go through their process. So I am not correct in saying that they did clear the FTC.

Senator METZENBAUM. I think on that point I ought to quit when I am ahead. My staff has pointed out and your staff has pointed out that that particular piece of information was not quite correct, but it was totally unintentional.

Mr. DILLER. It certainly was.

Senator METZENBAUM. We are grateful to have you be with us today, and we will say to you, as well as all others appearing before this subcommittee, we wish you well and we will see what happens.

Mr. DILLER. Thank you.

Senator METZENBAUM. Thank you very much.

Appendix E

TESTIMONY AND PREPARED STATEMENT OF DR. JOHN C. MALONE,
PRESIDENT AND CHIEF EXECUTIVE OFFICER, TELE-COMMUNICATIONS,
INC.

BEFORE THE

SUBCOMITTEE ON THE JUDICIARY
UNITED STATES SENATE

ONE HUNDRED THIRD CONGRESS

Senator METZENBAUM: I might say parenthetically that I agree with you, Senator Thurmond, that the trust of this hearing is not to litigate antitrust claims against TCI. That responsibility falls on another arm of government. Our responsibility is to explore the legal aspects from the standpoint of Congress and to explore the factual situation as well.

Mr. John Malone, president and chief executive officer of Tele-Communications. Inc., we are very happy to welcome you here this morning.

Statement('Testimony)Of John C. Malone

Mr. Malone. Thank you, Senator, for this opportunity to discuss with you the current situation. I am not particularly good at this, so I hope you indulge me.

I thought it would be useful to review a little history to put where TCI is today in context. This is our 25th anniversary as a public company. We started as a small group of entrepreneurs. We had a pretty consistent vision through these 25 years of what we wanted to do and how we wanted to succeed, and there were really two elements to that.

One was that by expanding viewing choice to customers, we could gain subscription. When we started, there were towns that had either no television at all or one or two channels. We built microwave systems and brought in additional programming choice. People liked that. That is how the industry started. We started with six-channel cable systems and we could only find three channels.

We also, as a founding theory, decided that we would go for growth; that we would, in fact, reinvest all available resources in growth; that we would pay low salaries; that we would compensate our employees by participation in the stock of the company, and that we would not pay dividends on that stock. We would just grow. We thought we were in a great growth industry even back then, and that by paying attention to these two fundamental issues we would create, in effect, sweat equity and could build a meaningful company.

In the early years, it was a very tough struggle. We were faced with programming largely controlled by very large enterprises, principally the broadcast networks, and they had a lot of political clout; we had none. From time to time, we were able to get the help of government, frankly, in freeing up restrictions and being able to add more and more choice to television viewing.

In order to technologically deliver these services, we had to continuously reinvest in technology and system capacity. So it became a very capital-intensive industry, one that had to be reinvented every 3 or 4 years, and we literally bootstrapped ourselves, adding channels, adding capacity, adding channels, adding capacity, gaining sub-scribers through a very tough period in the early 1970's.

In 1972, the FCC essentially blessed this philosophy, in fact, demanding that the cable industry originate its own programming. My company actually went out and made an investment in a marginal studio operation called Republic Pictures because we otherwise could not gain access to any programming. Unfortunately, that didn't turn out to be a particularly successful investment, but it did give us access to some old movies, some Westerns, some John Wayne movies, and so on, and we started the process of actually originating our own channels in 1972 and 1973.

Eventually, we succeeded. We innovated technology. We continued to stimulate programing. As our financial resources grew, as the size of our company grew, we were able to essentially identify through market research areas of programming that the public felt that they were underserved in.

For instance, one of the first investments we made in programming was Black Entertainment Television. We had won franchises in some metropolitan areas and we found that there was no targeted programming aimed at the black community. We financed an entrepreneur start-up, and after, I believe, 6 years of continuous losses he finally broke even, and that today is Black Entertainment Television, the public company. We continue to own, I believe, 16 percent of that company.

A little while after that, along came another opportunity to rescue Mr. Turner, my good friend, from financial ruin. He had overpaid-or let us put it this way: he had paid more than he could afford to pay for MGM and he was on the verge of having to liquidate his company or sell it to broadcasting interests. We felt it was far better for our customers and our business if we could raise capital and keep Mr. Turner independent. In all honestly, I have known Mr. Turner for a long while. Any indication that we can control Ted Turner is-three wives have tried and been unsuccessful.(Laughter.)

Just as silly, frankly, is the idea that we could control Barry Diller, one of the most gifted businessmen that I have ever met in my life.

As time has gone on, government has seen a need to adjust the regulatory rules. They did in 1972, they did it at various sequences. Generally, the FCC has been the point of action, but Congress acted in 1984 and many of the difficulties that we had that were headline-raising, these, let us say, aggressive fights between cities and cable operators, were put to bed by the 1984 legislation. It created a process for franchise renewal, a process which has actually worked quite well and has prevented the kind of very rending experiences that we had gone through previously.

Pursuing that strategy consistently, reinvesting, continuing to grow, has pretty well gotten us to be a successful enterprise, although we are not highly profitable at this point. In the last couple of years, I personally have thrown a lot of my time and attention into technology, which is my first love, and I was happy that the Congress passed the bill that allowed for joint industry R&D activities, which is an extremely useful antitrust exemption that allows an industry to get together, and identify its R&D needs and, in fact, develop technologies.

As chairman of Cable Labs, in the last few years I have been able to participate as the cable industry, I think, has led the charge into digital technologies for video applications. Relying on a lot of core American strengths and technologies, I believe that we successfully convinced the FCC to go to a 6 MHz processed digital high-definition television standard. When we lookb ack on that, that is going to turn out to be a landmark decision by the American Government because it creates a television standard that is American, that represents conservation of spectrum, and that really represents an explosion of choice and diversity in video distribution.

In the process of working in and around these technologies and this is really a converging thing. The computer industry, the communications industry, the cable industry and the broadcast industry on a worldwide basis are converging because of technology, because the digital technology is now making possible new things at lower cost than was ever dreamed of in the past.

These are technologies like optical fiber, micro circuits that we are talking about, micro processors, very sophisticated computer software techniques, distributed processing, systems engineering techniques that allow all of these things that we are talking about to, in effect, come into being. I think the societal benefits of the deployment of these technologies are enormous and I think well worthy of a lot of Government attention.

Clearly, job creation-we are talking about just the physical construction of these facilities generating about 100,000 direct jobs for at least 7 years just to get some of this stuff built. It will create an enormous export industry. This is an American technology. We are way in the lead, and the rest of the world that needs to upgrade its communications infrastructure is looking at this technology as ideal for deployment. We have the lead; we need to seize that lead. This can be an American industry worldwide, and once we have the industry in place, this can create an enormous export industry, a boom in the exportation of intellectual property entertainment programming, information programming, computer software; a huge potential business here.

From the consumer's point of view, this technology can empower the consumer. It can do exactly what Senator Kerrey asked for, give choice. It can make the consumer the boss, in effect. It really tears down all of the barriers, all of the limitations that we get accused of with our programming ownership. Essentially, there will be unlimited access to programming and services in this new architecture. The consumer is the boss. He can pick anything he wants really from his local supplier or from anyone else.

It is going to lead to efficiency in our society. It will make everything we do more efficient. The transportation of this information at these kinds of speeds will improve the efficiency of our industry. It will enhance productivity. The services that we talk about that we try and project the demand for-video on demand; random access to any movie or television show whenever you want to see it; video telephony, the ability to see your grandkids in very high quality at a very affordable price; broad-band telecommunications of all kinds; high-speed faxes, the ability to send high-quality photographs in very short order, which is very important in moving medical records around, things of that nature; all of the multimedia applications; interactivity on a client server basis. Instead of going into the yellow pages and calling a doctor at random, you are going to be able to go in and see who you can choose amongst, what their specialties are, and ever see a video clip of the doctor explaining to you their practice, their style of medicine, you get some sense of the personality of the physician. Those kinds of innovations are coming very fast.

Tele-commuting, the ability of people to work at home instead of having to commute to a central location-we have a large workforce now of customer service reps that work out of their homes. It expands employment to people who are handicapped.

The Internet phenomenon, which is, I know, a real phenomenon-we can extend Internet to the residences of America, broad-band Internet services, and that will lead to an explosion of computer networking and all of these other activities we are talking about.

PCs, incxpensive wireless communications bringing the power of cellular telephony to the masses at affordable prices, is just around the corner, and all kinds of interactive television, not just the kind of fun stuff, playing along with "Jeopardy" for small prizes, but being able to react Ross Perot when he asks you if it is a dumb idea or not-those kinds of things, real-time democracy, real-time feedback, all kinds of interactivity.

Probably the most important for our society long term is education both in the classroom and at home. These interactive technologies, I believe, will turn people from couch potatoes into full, participating students, in effect, in their homes and in the classrooms. Parents will be able to see what homework their kids are getting. They will be able to better support the education of their children. I think that area is really crucial for our society.

We can deliver textbooks at a fraction of the cost to inner-city schools that can't afford them. We can provide AP classes in rural schools where it would be impossible for those schools to afford the kind of teaching depth and curriculum otherwise available.

I think we can expect similar benefits in the health care area. We can do remote diagnosis of very high quality. Wherever you are in the country, if you have an emergency, your health records can be instantaneously available to the physician that serves you, and we can have high security in your access to the records.

Now, why do we need the Bell Atlantic deal? Some people think we are big and powerful and we have all these resources. The reality is we are pretty highly leveraged as a company. Yes, we are growing fast, and eventually we can do a lot of these things, but this opportunity is just too big for TCI on our own merits.

For one thing, we are entering a world of giant competitors. We have got revenues of less than $4 billion a year. AT&T isn't big enough, we have got foreign telephone companies, many of them state-owned, competing directly with us both domestically here and in international markets.

Senator METZENBAUM. How much more time do you need, Mr. Malone?

Mr. MALONE. About 2 minutes.

Senator METZENBAUM. Take 5 minutes if you need it. I don't want to press you.

Mr. MALONE. I think it is important to state that the three things that TCI really lacks to pursue this future on our own-we don't have the political skills necessary, in all sincerity. We don't have the financial depth, the depth of our balance sheet, to go head to head with the size companies. Finally, we don't have the people to execute a telephony entry strategy in any real-time sense. We need to rely on a strategic partner for that.

I think this deal assures competition. I think it assures that in our markets we will be offering telephony service-"we" being Bell Atlantic, will be offering telephony services against the incumbent telephone company, and they will undoubtedly align with other telephone companies to provide telephone service against Bell Atlantic. So we see this leading to an almost immediate duopoly, if you want to call it that, immediate competition in terms of the full array of full-service network services.

Finally, we understand this is a massive activity. The convergence of communications-computer, telephone, cable is a huge activity in our society. We understand Government's concern. We hope to work with the Congress closely in satisfying any concerns that the Congress has and structuring the relationship to accommodate those concerns.

We really believe in competition. We believe we have to become competitive. We believe it is becoming a very competitive world. I believe today Hughes launched the direct broadcast satellite that will offer national broadcast service of all the cable channels directly against the incumbent cable industry. So it is getting very competitive, but we have an enormous opportunity not only domestically, but internationally, and we are just not big enough to pursue this and that is why we want the alignment with Bell Atlantic.

Prepared Statement Of John C. Malone

Mr. Chairman, members of the Subcommittee, my name is John Malone. I am the President and Chief Executive Officer of Tele-Communications, Inc.("TCI").

I appreciate the opportunity to come before you this morning to talk about our company's merger with Bell Atlantic and about our vision of the future. I regret that I was unable to join my colleague Ray Smith when he appeared before you earlier this year. I appreciate the Subcommittee's willingness to accommodate my schedule by giving me this chance to come before you today.

I would like to discuss briefly how TCI got to where it is today and where it is I believe we are headed. I would also like to offer the Subcommittee my views on some of the competition policy issues that have been brought to your attention. Then I will attempt to answer your questions.

I. TCI-THE GROWTH AND EVOLUTION

Sparked by dramatic increases in the processing and storage capacity of tiny computer chips, an enormous revolution in the way Americans communicate with one another is now underway. Our children routinely will use an array of competing communications networks to control thousands of video, data and telephone options that promise a richer, more productive and satisfying life for all. From our childrens' perspective, I am certain the first bold steps we are now taking in otical fiber, digital television, video switching and related technologies will be recognized as the dawning of the Information Age.

This is a revolution from within. The President and Vice President of the United States, the latter with particular effectiveness, have heralded its coming and established the information superhighway as a critical national objective. Leaders in Congress have pledged their support and are now drafting the regulatory ground rules under which it will operate.

The private sector has responded by committing billions to the construction of full service networks and services that will appear on them. Companies such as AT&T and McCaw, USWest and Time Warner, and Southwestern Bell and Cox, Bell Canada and Jones Intercable, and Bell Atlantic and my company are organizing themselves to build a new national Infostructure that will bring several of them in direct head-to-head competition with one another.

No sector of our nation's economy holds more promise or commands greater excitement today than the telecommunications industry. Yet, it would be foolish for any one person or company to take credit for these developments. Rather it is the working of a free and entrepreneurial marketplace, where companies and combinations of companies are rushing to be first, that has made the difference.

Most of the telecommunications giants that are involved can trace their lineage back o the turn of the century or before, but our company TCI is only 25 years old this year. Neither the Congress, the press nor many customers took much notice in 1968 when Bon Magness, our Chairman and Founder, turned his back on the cottonseed business forever and started TCI. Few cared as we flirted with insolvency for many months before and after my arrival as CEO of the company in 1972. Our obscurity was well-earned in those days as we struggled long hours with the fundamentals of our business.

Most of those who went through those tortured first years with Bon and me are still with our company today. Few recognized that the rough trails we blazed in those days would be guideposts for the information superhighway of tomorrow.

However, I am pleased to say the business principles that guided us as we achieved financial stability then are the same ones that guide us today, and the ones that will be the foundation for the merged Bell Atlantic and TCI.

First, we will continue to be agents of change. For most of us, television 25 years ago was three or four local VHF broadcast channels. Today, we have ten times the number of choices and, in many cities, more. Premium and pay-per-view channels provide additional markets for movie studios, and we even have more broadcast choices, since cable has extended the reach of hundreds of UHF broadcast stations making them economically viable.

The compressed digital systems we will begin to deploy next year represent the first step in giving our customers even more choice and more control over their television service. Within three years, we will be deploying interactive full service networks with powerful computing devices in the home to give customers random access to stored and real time video programming, data and telephone products.

Certainly, everyone in the television business is not advantaged by change. Some of those who have dominated television for forty years are outright opposed and, regrettably, they have occasionally gained allies in the Congress.

However, the dramatic pace of technological development has made change inevitable. Our philosophy has been to lead in some areas, to follow in others, but to seek acceleration of change on nearly every front. We know change is likely to bring our customers more choice and control over their television service.

A second principle that has served us well is our view that we are purchasing agents for our customers. Basically, we purchase video programming wholesale and sell it retail. If wholesale prices can be maintained at a reasonable level, our customers pay less for cable service.

Despite our best efforts, programming costs have escalated dramatically over the last five years several hundred percent in our case although much of that can be accounted for by significant increases in the quality of cable programming.

Nevertheless, we bargain hard with our programmers, and occasionally the resulting frictions have been brought to the attention of Congress. Most Members have been reluctant to interfere in such commercial disputes, especially when they are reflected in litigation, but there have been exceptions.

A third principle has been constant reinvestment in our business. At TCI, we do not pay dividends to our shareholders and we have never reported material annual earnings during the entire 25 years of our existence. Excess cash flow goes back into our systems and into additional programming. As detailed later, we have often invested in socially responsible programing such as the Discovery Channel and Black Entertainment Television, when no one else would. We also have invested millions in education technology-$300,000 alone in the 10 percent of Ohio's schools that we serve.

A related principle has been a relatively purer form of entrepreneurial management. We have attempted to remain lean and flexible. Although many of our employees have done well at TCI, including me, that has come through appreciation of our share values, not because of unreasonable high salaries or bonuses. We have an ESOP, in which many of our employees participate.

The changes that our full service networks will bring to our nation will enhance virtually all the public policy objectives traditionally within the interest of this Subcommittee. In some cases, the companies will be larger, but we will see a dramatic increase in the number of large companies competing with each other. We already see evidence of this within 10 miles of where we sit today. Southwestern Bell and Bell Canada have purchased cable systems in Montogomery County and Arlington that will compete directly against Bell Atlantic/TCI. Ultimately, our interest in the cable system here in D.C. will be divested to a Bell Atlantic competitor, should our merger be approved.

Even more importantly, development of full service networks will ignite an explosion of entrepreneurial concerns which will develop competing video, data and telephone applications for the new networks. It will be in the best business interest of competing network providers to nurture these companies by allowing open and easy access to the ultimate customer.

The impact of all these developments on the customer will be most profound.

First, we foresee a dramatic increase in the choices available to the viewing public. Consumers will have many more entertainment, news, and sports options, but there also will be available a range of educational, shopping, work-at-home, energy, management, and other services that will change the way we live our lives.

By the end of this decade, many Americans could have four or more providers of multi-channel video services and two or more telephone providers. Thus, we will not only see a huge increase in the number and variety of services, but also an order of magnitude increase in the number of companies that offer them.

Second, consumers will have more control over their television service. The electronics and service platform we and others are developing will empower consumers to personalize their service and use tomorrow's television as a device to make their lives easier. If we can win cooperation from the programmers, we will have systems which allow consumers to take and pay for only those services they want when they want them.

The third element of our strategic vision is consumer convenience. With the complexity of our evolving networks and the plethora of choices they will offer, our customers must have on-screen guides and gateway devices that help them travel the information superhighway.

I believe, Mr. Chairman, that neither you nor your Subcommittee will argue about the merits of building our nation's Infostructure. I also believe that what I have said above the more traditional competition policy analysis that follows later in my testimony will convince objective observers that the combination of TCI and Bell Atlantic, assuming the divestiture of in-region cable assets, should not raise any significant antitrust concerns.

You certainly have heard your share of anecdotes from previous witnesses, all of which have been discussed at length here and in other body when Congress debated and passed the Cable Act of 1992 over the President's veto. The Congress designed many, complex provisions in the 1992 Act to deal with these situations and others like them involving other companies.

Many of those Cable Act provisions are just now taking effect. Others will take effect soon in accordance with timetables established by Congress just last year. To suggest now that all these issues be revisited before the 1992 Act has even been fully implemented makes no sense at all.

Without getting into details, I can assure you that virtually all these anecdotes are either completely untrue or wildly inflated by business competitors who seek your help in gaining commercial advantage.

However, I do believe there is a basic issue of trust that you and your Subcommittee Members are pondering. I realize it is part of your job to gain some comfort with the motivations of those involved in major national enterprises as important as the Information Superhighway. I also realize that I have become a target for a wide range of business competitors and consumer lobbyists who are dissatisfied with the pace of change in our industry, the first believing it to be too fast and the second believing it to be too slow.

I regret that neither I nor my company can ever respond to this type of controversy in ways that Washington normally expects.

For myself, I will continue to resist the notion that I need to sacrifice my privacy in order to respond to public misrepresentations about my motivations. Becoming a "public figure" means unacceptable risks to the health, safety, and privacy of my family, and I will continue to refuse most of the hundreds of requests for press interviews to "tell my side of the story."

With respect to TCI, we simply are not going to spend anywhere near the many millions spent y other companies on public relations, image advertising or government affairs. Instead, we know our customers prefer we spend scarce resources on our cable systems and new programming.

We do respect the role of government, we do our best to comply with its laws and regulations, and we willingly supply factual information to panels such as yours that are conducting legitimate inquiries.

Nor am I suggesting that every negative comment about TCI or me is a public relations or competitive ploy We have been building a brand new industry where the rules are not well established. We make our share of mistakes, but when we do, we try to correct them and move on.

Moving now to the specific subject of these hearing, it has been apparent to informed observers for some time that the current structure of the telephone and cable industries is inadequate to finish construction of the nation's Infostructure before the end of this century. Once technological development reached a critical stage and once government identified the Information Superhighway as a critical national objective, the types of business combination that are now being announced almost weekly became inevitable.

The problem, simply put, is that no one cable or telephone company has the financial resources or combination of skills to do the job. It will cost at least $60 billion to give existing cable and telephone networks the capability of carrying broadband, two-way interactive video programming and to equip subscribers to participate in these networks. Moreover, the task requires a thorough knowledge of national network operations, computer applications and the video marketplace that few, if any, companies now have.

Thus, we believe mergers and joint ventures, like the proposed Bell Atlantic/TCI merger, should be approved with, where necessary, appropriate regulatory safeguards. In the case of our merger, Bell Atlantic's stated intention to divest itself of in-region TCI cable operations within its telephone service area should be sufficient to meet any objective antitrust standard, as it was in the case of the USWest investment in Time Warner's cable operations.

II. TCI In Perspective

A. TCI and Size

Mr. Chairman, much of what I have discussed so far is of concern to all of the Members of Congress, and rightfully so. These developments in telecommunications may prove to be of unparalleled importance and they deserve your review and scrutiny.

I know the particular focus of this Subcommittee is the protection and promotion of competition for the benefit of consumers. That is what the antitrust laws, of course, are all about. Although I would prefer to focus on the dynamic challenges we are prepared to face, and the tremendous contributions to society and the economy that will come from meeting those challenges, I feel compelled to address at least in general some of the unprincipled and undeserved accusation that other witnesses before this Subcommittee have leveled at TCI and at me personally. Some of these accusations are the substance of pending litigation and I am limited in the way I can deal with them in this format. However, I believe it may be useful for the Subcommittee if I offer some general observations that will put some of these baseless charges into perspective.

If I relied solely on recent press stories to learn about TCI and the role that it plays in the entertainment and information industry. I would think that I was dealing with an entity combining the power of the pre-divestiture AT&T, IBM when it was the only name in computers, and the U.S. Postal Service before anyone ever heard of UPS or Federal Express. However effective these media images may be as political or competitive propaganda, they are simply not accurate, and indeed are dangerous distortions of the truth.

First, let's get the table set correctly. TCI is a large company, but we are certainly not a giant, whether compared to other telecommunications and technology firms or American companies as a whole. TCI's 1992 revenues(including Liberty)were a little over $3.7 billion. By comparison, AT&T and IBM each had 1992 revenues of over $65 billion; indeed, AT&T had higher profits($3.8 billion)in 1992 than TCI's total revenues. In the telecommmications area alone, TCI is dwarfed by, among others, all of the regional telephone operating companies(whose 1992 revenues ranged from $10 to 15 billion each); GTE, with 1992 revenues $19.9 billion; Time Warner, with revenues of $13 billion; and MCI, withe revenues of over $10 billion. Even combined with Bell Atlantic, the resulting company could be only 15 percent as large as a combined AT&T/McCaw.

Video programming is delivered to American consumers by a variety of mechanisms, including cable. Any proper measure of concentration would have to take account of all those alternatives, including over-the-air broadcasters, video cassette sales and rentals, MMDS, SMATV and(soon)DBS. But even ignoring all that, and looking just at cable, the business is unconcentrated in both absolute and relative terms. Chart 1 shows the relative concentration levels of various industries-again limiting video distribution to cable operators. Cable is clearly the least concentrated, significantly below the 1000 level that the federal antitrust agencies describe as the level below which markets are not concentrated. There are 13 cable operators who serve at least one million subscribers, but there are only six major movie studios and just four broadcast television networks.

CHART 1: HHI MEASURES OF INDUSTRY CONCENTRATION	
Cable Television System Ownership	[1]623
Domestic Theatrical Motion Picture Revenues	[2]1577
Prime Time Television Viewing	[3]1430
Long Distance Carriers' Toll Revenues	[4]3938

[1]Kagan, Cable Television Developments, November 1993
[2]Variety, January 11, 1993
[3]Broadcasting & Cable, December 13, 1993
[4]FCC News, October 5, 1993

In addition, TCI is hardly a dominant company by any conventual standards, even in this artificially small "market." As Chart 2 shows, TCI/Liberty serves only about 20 percent of U.S. cable subscribers. [30] By comparison, AT&T still enjoys more than 60 percent of long distance revenues, and Nintendo makes over 75 percent of video games system sales.

Moreover, cable activities alone are clearly not the appropriate measure of TCI's relative size, since many noncable firms compete directly with cable companies, including TCI. At an absolute minimum, TCI's direct competitors include all firms that provide video programming to consumers; they purchase programming, not delivery mechanisms. The list of such competitors is already long-video rental stores, wireless cable, over-the-air broadcasters, SMATV operators and backyard dish dealers-and will grow longer in 1994 with the addition of a new delivery option(high power direct broadcast satellites)and new(and well-funded)industry participants-DirecTV(owned by Hughes, a General Motors subsidiary)and United

---

[30]As Chart 2 shows, cable systems in which TCI or Liberty owns at least a majority of the outstanding stock serve 10.7 million basic subscribers. If those subscribers served by systems that are not majority owned but are managed by TCI are added, the total basic subscribers number increases to 11.2 million. The addition of basic subscribers served by all other cable systems in which TCI or Liberty have an investment interest, but does not manage, increases the total to 13.4 million.

States Satellite Broadcasting(owned by Hubbard Broadcasting, a radio and television pioneer).

CHART 2: TCI/LIBERTY OWNED AND/OR MANAGED CABLE SYSTEMS		
TCI/Liberty	Homes Passed[1] (millions)	Basic Subscribers (millions)
Majority owned	18.8 (20.6%)	10.7 (18.9%)
Majority owned plus managed systems	19.6 (21.4%)	11.2 (19.8%)
TCI/Liberty total	23.8 (26.0%)	13.4 (23.7%)
National total	91.4	56.5

[1]All percentages based on estimates of National Total Homes Passed and Basic Subscribers for August 1993, from Paul Kagan Associates, Inc. "Marketing New Media." August 16, 1993, p. 3. As reported in MCTA Cable Television Developments, November 1993.

When viewed in light of the approximately $200 billion in annual spending on entertainment(even excluding live entertainment), TCI's annual revenues are insignificant-less than 2 percent. Looking just at video programming, Chart 3 shows that TCI's total revenues are less than half of that generated by video cassette and rentals alone-approximately $8 billion in 1992. Adding video rental revenues(and ignoring video cassette sales and all other competing video distributors)to total cable revenues, TCI's supposedly "dominant" share would fall to 12 percent. [31]

This is simply not a dominant position by any traditional analysis. Of course, those with a political or competitive agents, like Mr. Redstone in your earlier hearings,

---

[31]Chart 3 shows two calculations: TCI's basic and pay cable revenues as a percent of total basic cable, pay cable and video cassette rental revenues; and TCI's total revenues as a percent of all cable subscriber revenues and video cassette rental revenues. In both cases, TCI's "share" is essentially the same-11-12 percent. Of course, even this calculation is conservative, because it ignores all other video distributors and video cassette sales, which are obviously directly competitive alternatives and all other entertainment options.

recognize this reality and frequently try to augment these modest numbers by ignoring video sales and rentals and by attributing to TCI the subscribers served by other cable firms such as Comcast, Cox, or Newhouse, which have occasionally joined with TCI in programming investments or other ventures. This aggregation, of course, is totally inappropriate, since neither TCI nor Liberty has any ownership interest in any of these companies nor any involvement in the operations or management of their cable systems. The plain facts are that TCI is simply the largest, but hardly dominant, firm in an unconcentrated industry, and all the overblown rhetoric to the contrary is simply hot air.

CHART 3: 1992 CABLE SUBSCRIBER REVENUE AND VIDEO RENTAL REVENUES	
Cable subscriber revenues	
Basic revenues	$13,261
Pay revenues	4,930
Total[1]	21,694
Video cassette rental revenues	8,224
Total Basic Cable, Pay Cable, and video cassette rental revenues	26,415
All cable subscriber revenues and video cassette rental revenues	29,918
TCI Basic Cable and Pay Cable revenues	2,945
Total TCI revenues	3,574
TCI Basic and Pay Cable reveneus as a percent of total Basic Cable, and video cassette rental revenue	11%
TCI total revenues as a percent of all cable subscriber revenues and video cassette rental revenues	12%

[1] Includes revenues from installation, expanded basic service, advertising, additional charges, rental contracts, etc.
Source: RCTA, Cable Television Developments, November 1993, Video Software Dealers Association.

Finally, I cannot emphasize too strongly how wrong it is for anyone to speak of TCI "controlling" its subscribers. TCI has no "control" over anyone. Only slightly over half of those who we offer cable services to actually buy those services-a figure comparable to the industry as a whole. Obviously, each of these potential subscribers has a large number of other suppliers vying for their entertainment dollars, and most have several different alternatives for the delivery of video programming, including various combinations of over-the-air broadcasters, video sales and rentals, wireless cable(MMES.), back-yard dishes, SMATV operators and, beginning in 1994, at least two high power DBS distributors. In the foreseeable future, many of these potential subscribers will have another choice-programming delivered over telephone wires. Given this extensive competition just for video programming, not to mention other entertainment alternatives, it makes as much sense to speak of TCI "controlling" its subscribers as it does to speak of the broadcast networks "controlling" the audience that dials in the local channel that carries their programming.

B. TCI and Programming

The myth of TCI "control" over cable programming is particularly annoying to me, both when advanced by those with a competitive ax to grind and even more so when accepted uncritically by policy makers. We are proud of the role we have played in creating and preserving important and useful programming. We have not supported so-called "adult" programming or programming that glorifies violence or antisocial behavior. Instead, we have invested in otherwise supported financially services like The Discovery Channel, The Learning Channel, Court TV, Black Entertainment Television, VISN/ACTS, and The Family Channel, in addition to the Turner services. We have been selective in our investments; we probably get as many as 20 programming proposals a month, and our focus in making investments has been to provide attractive programming choices to our subscribers.

Indeed, the history of the cable investors or financiers of last resort for cable programmers. The founders of Black Entertainment Television(Robert Johnson)and The Discovery Channel(John Hendricks)both have described on numerous occasions the difficulties they have encountered in obtaining funding for their infant, and financially struggling, services. After they had been repeatedly turned down by other investment sources, cable operators provided financing that ensured the continued survival of the services and made possible their present success. As a result, Bob Johnson has stated that, through its financial support of BET, the cable industry has "done more to create minority programming and diversity in television than all FCC regulations and broadcasting outreach programs combined."[32]

Such actions have contributed significantly to the present range and diversity of programming choices.[33] Before the development of the modern cable industry, consumers' viewing choices were limited to the three broadcast networks, PBS and a few independent broadcast sttions. In just over twenty years, in addition to the growth of UHF independents, more than 70 satellite-delivered national programming services have developed, with numerous specialty channels devoted to childrens programming, minority programming, the arts, and public affairs, and a growing number of regional news and sports services.

The financial contributions of cable operators like TCI were important forces leading to this explosion in consumer choice. The FCC recognized the benefits of integration in its 1990 analysis of the cable industry, where it concluded, based on an extensive record: "[T]his vertical integration has increased both quality and the quantity of programming services available to the viewing public." Rate Deregulation and the Commission's Policies Relating to the Provision of Cable Television Service, 5 F.C.C. Red. 4962, 5007(1990). The FCC reaffirmed this conclusion this year:

As Congress recognized, and the record in this proceeding confirms, there are significant benefits to cable subscribers which result from vertical integration. First, MSO investment in cable programming services has provided cable subscribers with a variety of high quality cable programming services.

---

[32]See Media Ownership: Diversity an d Concentration: Hearings before the Subcomm. On Communications of Comm. on Commerce, Science and Transportation, 101st Congress, 1st Session 211(1989)(Statement of Robert L. Johnson).

[33]As Viacom noted in its comments to the FCC on implementing the Cable Act of 1992: "Multichannel video distributors in general, and cable operators in particular, have been at the forefront of developing new program services. To preclude such cable operator participation could result in decreased diversity by foreclosing new program services." Comments of Viacom International Inc. in MM Docket No. 92-264(Feb. 9, 1993)at 20.

Appendix F

The Antitrust Laws And Theories Of Their Enforcement

John D. Rockefeller's Standard Oil Trust overwhelming market power and market domination and several of its imitators in the 1880s generated formidable opposition among small-business owners, farmers, and the public against monopoly, resulting in the antitrust laws. The laws were so named because of the method of corporate consolidation in the late nineteenth century. Briefly, owners of stock of competing organizations transferred legal title to a group of trustees and received certificates in return. The trustees then the exercised working control over the firms as a single firm. The two basic pillars of the laws were,(1)The Sherman Act of 1890, and(2)The Clayton Act and the Federal Trade Commission(FTC)Act of 1914[34]

THE SHERMAN ACT

The two most significant sections of this Act are 1 and 2. Section 1 reads: "Every contract, combination in the form of trust or otherwise, or conspiracy, in restraint of trade or commerce among the several states, or with foreign nations, is hereby declared to be illegal." Section 2 reads: "Every person who shall monopolize, or attempt to monopolize, or combine or conspire with any person or persons, to monopolize any part of the trade or commerce among the several states, or with foreign nations, shall be deemed guilty of a misdemeanor, and, on conviction therefore, shall be punished by fine."[35] Section 1 has applicability to agreements involving two or more people, whereas Section 2 is broader and involves individual attempts to monopolize. However, adverse rulings of the Court, coupled with lax administation led to dissatisfaction of

---

[34]George A. Steiner, and John F. Steiner, Business, Governent, and Society: A Managerial Perspective, Eighth ed.,(McGraw-Hill, New York, 1997), 307-308.

[35]Ibid., 308.

the operation of the Act, and raised demands for more exact definitions of illegal monopolistic practices intended by the Act.[36]

THE CLAYTON ACT AND THE FEDERAL
TRADE COMMISSION(FTC)ACT

This Act sought to identify specific monopolistic behaviors which were illegal under the law. Realizing that laws without enforcement are no laws, the FTC Act was passed alongside to ensure supervision and administration of the antitrust laws, so as to end "unfair methods of competition in commerce, and unfair or deceptive acts or practices in commerce..." [Section 5(a)with a modification by the Wheeler-Lea Act of 1938]. The Acts are long and their language is frequently unclear. For example, in Section 7 it is explicitly stated that no firm can acquire another where the effect is to substantially limit competition between the two companies or to create a monopoly of any line of commerce. The Department of Justice is entrusted with the authority to enforce the Sherman Act and jurisdiction over the Clayton Act cases is shared between the department and the FTC.[37]

THEORIES IN THE ENFORCEMENT
OF THE ANTITRUST LAWS

A Supreme Court opinion pertaining to the Sherman Act better epitomizes the intent of

the Antitrust Laws:

The Sherman Act was designed to be a comprehensive charter of economic liberty aimed at preserving free and unfettered competition as the rule of trade. It rests on the premise that the unrestrained interaction of competitive forces will yield the best allocation of our economic resources, the lowest

---

[36]Ibid.
[37]Ibid., 308-309.

prices, the highest quality, and the greatest material progress, while at the same time providing an environment conducive to the preservation of our demo- cratic political and social institutions. But even were that premise open to question, the policy unequivocally laid down by the Act is competition.[38]

This opinion of the Supreme Court reinforces the three cornerstone of the capitalist system-economic, social, and political. Economic is, of course, very obvious. Social, because it emphasizes the greater welfare for individuals, or consumers. Political because it lays much stress on political democracy by restraining concentrated economic power that can seriously present distorting influence on democratic principles. Seeking to arrive at this basic objective has led to two major theories of enforcement, being the "Structuralist" and the "Performance" theories.[39]

THE STRUCTURALIST THEORY

In this theory, the Court's sole perception, until recently, was that corporate size and large market share are a reliable measure of monopoly power in its interpretations of the Antitrust Laws. The typical index of power is concentration of assets or sales of one or a few firms in an industry. Concentration is determimed as the ratio of sales and/or assets of the entire industry. This theory contends that too much concentration of market power gives corporate managers discretionary power to fix prices, determine which products come to market, and in what quantity, and amass tremendous prof- its. That, too much market power produces price inflation, production inefficiencies, and injury to competition. Adherents of this theory further argue that to assure the well-being of competition, a break up of concentration of economic power and/or preventing such concentration from developing is very necessary(see Appendix B, the

---

[38]U.S. v. Northern Pacific Railroad Company, 356 U.S. 1(1958), quoted in George A. Steiner, and John F. Steiner, Business, Government, and Society: A Managerial Perspective, Eighth ed.,(McGraw-Hill, New York, 1997), 309.
[39]Ibid.

argument of Sumner Redstone). This theory has been advocated by economists for many years, and expounded in their academic research.[40]

THE PERFORMANCE THEORY

This theory, which emerged relatively recently, contends that public policy should search for appropriate market structures in addition to efficient business performance. It argues that efficient business performance guarantees product and process innovation, cost reduction and its attendant beneficial effects to the consumer in terms of lower prices, productive capacity that balances product demand, profits in keeping with other industries, and lays emphasis on service to the consumer. It further argues that the assertion that concentration hinders competition is flawed, especially, in these days of powerful global competition because, the concentration ratio is diminished significantly when global competition is taken into account. For example, the production of jet engines is quite high in the U.S., but when sales of foreign manufacturers are brought into the picture, the concentration ratio diminishes significantly.[41]

---

[40]Ibid., 309-310.

[41]Ibid., 310.

Glossary

Acquiring company(Acquirer)-A company that seeks to acquire another company.

Acquisition-An economic event in which one firm acquires a controlling interest in another firm, which continues to exist as a separate legal entity.

Amortization-The process of systematically allocating a cost to expense over a period of time.

Common stock-The ownership rights of investors in a corporation.

Congeneric merger-A merger of companies in the same general industry, but for which no customer or supplier relationship exists.

Conglomerate merger-A merger of firms in totally different industries.

Corporate alliance-A cooperative deal that falls short of a merger.

Corporation(Incorporation)-A legal entity separate and distinct from its owners.

Defensive merger-A merger designed to make a firm less vulnerable to a takeover.

Debt financing-Results when a company obtains financial resources from creditors.

Discontinued operation-Major lines of business or segments from which a company will no longer derive income.

Divestiture-The sale of a firm's operating assets.

Dividends-Distributions of assets, usually cash, to stockholders from a corporation's profits.

Earnings per share-A measure of earnings performance of share of common stock during a fiscal period; computed by dividing net income by the average number of shares of common stock outstanding during a fiscal period.

Equity financing-The issuance of stock as a means of raising capital for a corporation.

Financial merger-A merger in which the companies involved will not be operated as a single unit and from which no operating economies are expected.

Fiscal period-Any period of time for which operating results are collected and reported; could be a day, week, month, quarter, year, etc.

Fixed costs-Expenses that do not vary in proportion to sales activity.

Form 10-K reports-Annual registration statement filled by corporations with the Securities and Exchange Commission(SEC).

Friendly merger-A merger whose terms are approved by the management of both companies.

Holding company-A firm that owns sufficient common stock of another firm to achieve working control of it.

Horizontal merger-A combination of two companies that produce the same type of good or service.

Hostile merger-A merger in which the target company's management resists acquisition.

Information-Facts, ideas, and concepts that help us understand the world.

Intangible assets-Long-term legal rights resulting from the ownership of patents, copyrights, trademarks, and similar items.

Investors-Owners and creditors who provide money to an organization with the expectation of earning a return.

Liquid assets-Resources that can be converted to cash in a relatively short period.

Liquidity-The extent to which an organization has sufficient cash and other liquid assets to pay current obligation.

Market-Any location or process that permits the exchange of resources.

Marketable security-A financial instrument(usually a stock or bond)that can be readily sold in an organized market.

Merger-An economic event that occurs when companies combine their resources and operations so only one legal entity continues to exist.

Operating activities-The use of resources to design, produce, distribute, and market goods and services.

Operating merger-A merger in which operations of the firms involved are integrated in hope of achieving synergistic benefits.

Organization-A group of people who work together to develop, produce, and/or distribute goods or services.

Outstanding shares-The number of a corporation's shares currently held by investors.

Parent company-A holding company; a company which controls another company by owning more than 50% of the other company's common stock.

Preferred stock-Stock that has a higher claim on dividends and assets than common stock.

Profit-The difference between the price received for goods or services sold and the total cost to the seller of all resources consumed in developing, producing, and selling those goods or services during a particular period; another name for net income or net earnings.

Profit margin-The ratio of a company's earnings to its operating revenues, it is a measure of the ability of a company to generate profits from its sales.

Proxy-A document that authorizes management to cast votes for its stockholders at a stockholder's meeting.

Proxy statement-Information distributed to stockholders about matters that will be considered at a corporation's annual stockholder's meeting.

Return on investment-The amount of profit earned by a business that could be paid to owners.

Revenues-Increases in assets or decreases in liabilities from selling goods or providing services that constitute the primary activities of an organization.

Spin-off-A divestiture in which the stock of a subsidiary is given to the parent company's stockholders.

Stock-Certificates of ownership in a corporation.

Stockholders-Owners of a corporation.

Stock market-An organization established to facilitate the trading of shares of corporate securities; examples include the New York Stock Exchange, the American Stock Exchange, or the Tokyo Stock Exchange.

Subsidiary-A corporation controlled by other corporations, normally by ownership of more than 50% of the subsidiary's common stock.

Synergy-The condition wherein the whole is greater than the sum of its parts; in a synergistic merger, the postmerger value exceeds the sum of the separate firms' premerger values.

Target company-A company that another company seeks to acquire.

Tender office-The offer of one company to buy the stock of another by going directly to the stockholders, frequently(but not always)over the opposition of the target company's management.

Transaction-An event that increases or decreases an account balance.

Two-tier offer-A merger offer which provides different(better)terms to those who tender their stock earliest.

Variable costs-Expenses that vary in proportion to sales activity.

Vertical merger-A merger between a company and one of its suppliers or customers.

White knight-A firm that is more acceptable to the management of a company under attack in a hostile takeover attempt.

Bibliography

Books

Brigham, E. F. *Financial Management*. Hinsdale, Illinois: The Dryden Press, 1985.

Daniels, Peggy Kneffel, and Susan E. Edgar, eds. *Job Seeker's Guide*. The Northeast. Detroit: Gale Research International Ltd., 1995.

Gaughan, Patrick A. *Mergers, Acquisitions and Corporate Restructurings*. New York: John Wiley and Sons, Inc., 1996

Glueck, W. F. *Business Policy and Strategic Management*. New York: McGraw-Hill Book Company, 1984.

Miles, Raymond C. *Basic Business Appraisal*. New York: John Wiley and Sons, 1984.

————. *How To Price A Business*. Englewood Cliffs, New Jersey: Institute for Business Planning, 1985.

Robinson, David. *The History of World Cinema*. New York: Stein and Day, 1981.

Scharf, Charles A., Edward E. Shea, George C. Beck. *Acquisitions, Mergers, Sales, Buyouts, and Takeovers: A Handbook with Forms*. Englewood Cliffs, New Jersey: Prentice Hall, 1995.

Sudarsanam, P. S. *The Essence of Mergers and Acquisitions*. Cornwall, United Kingdom: Prentice Hall, 1995.

Weston, Fred J., and Eugene F. Brigham. *Essentials of Managerial Finance*. New York: The Dryden Press, 1993.

Articles

Bates, James. "Paramount Deal." *Los Angeles Times,* 16 February 1994, A16.

Chatterjeu, S. "Types of Synergy and Economic Value: The Impact of Acquisitions on Merging and Rival Firms." *Strategic Management Journal 7,* 1986, 119-139.

Comte, Elizabeth. "Giving Viewers A Choice." *Forbes,* 4 January 1993, 142.

Drucker, P.F. "The Problem of Corporate Takeovers: What Is to Be Done?" *The Public Interest,* Winter 1986, 20.

"Foreign Investors Bought Fewer U.S. Assets Last Year." *Forbes,* 23 July 1990, 146.

Freund, James C., and Richard L. Easton. "The Three-Piece Suitor: An Alternative Approach to Negotiated Corporate Acquisitions." *The Thirteenth Forum on Negotiating Corporate Acquisitions.* New York: Law Journal Seminars-Press, 1989, 25-36.

————-. "Viacom, Inc." *Value Line Investment Survey,* 25 March 1994, 386.

Gerstein, Marc. "Paramount Communications." *Value Line Investment Survey,* 4 March 1994, 17767.

La Franco, Robert. "Entertainment and Information." *Forbes,* 12 January 1998, 148-149.

Pennar, Karen. "This Dwarf Recession Might be a Giant." *Business Week,* 15 October 1990, 30.

Securities and Exchange Commission. *Annual Report of Viacom Inc.(10-K)for the Fiscal Year Ended December 31, 1996.* Washington, D.C

Sharav, Ben. "Entertainment Industry" *Value Line Investment Survey.* 1997. 30 May, 1778, 28 November, 1787, 1789.

Smith, George S. Jr., Vaughan A. Clark, and Christina Hornbeck. "Viacom Reports First Quarter 1997 Revenues of $2.9 billion, EBITDA of $392 million and Operating Income of $174 million." *News From Viacom,* 7 May 1997, 1.

"The M & A Watch: Is This Any Way To Run A Company?" *Financial Executive,* April 1988, 1, 3-4.

Tucker, Timothy F. "QVC Network." *Value Line Investment Survey,* 25 February 1994,.1705.

U.S. Census Bureau Report, Series H 121-90-2. *Home Ownership Trends in the 1980's*. Washington: U.S. Government Printing Office, 1990.

U.S. Mergers & Acquisitions magazine, Vol. 29/Number 1, July/August 1994, 76.

THE NEW YORK TIMES

New York Times. 1993. 10, 11 September. 1998. 22 January.

WALL STREET JOURNAL

Wall Street Journal. 1994. 14, 15, 16 February; 16 March. 1996. 22 January; 15 April; 6 May; 25 June: 9 July; 1,5 August; 16 December.

www.ingramcontent.com/pod-product-compliance
Lightning Source LLC
Chambersburg PA
CBHW030949180526
45163CB00002B/712